Thanksgiving

My Dear Daughter Sandra,

So often we fail to
thank the Lord for the
many blessings we
recieve and enjoy in our
busy life.

I am truly thankful for
you as a loving, caring
daughter, wife and mother.

I love you very much
and know that the Lord
will bless you always.
you are truly a Spirit
of the Lord.

My love,
Dad

Variable Clouds, Occasional Rain, with a Promise of Sunshine

Variable Clouds, Occasional Rain, *with a* Promise *of* Sunshine

Paul H. Dunn

BOOKCRAFT
Salt Lake City, Utah

Library of Congress Catalog Card Number: 86-71162
ISBN 0-88494-599-5

5th Printing, 1987

Printed in the United States of America

Contents

Preface

It has often been said that "into each life some rain must fall." A popular blues song warns us of "stormy weather," and nightly our weather reports on the news tell of occasional clouds, approaching storms, and the eventual sunshine we all seek.

Life, like the weather, has its "gloomy days" filled with many challenges. Altogether too many people are defeated by the everyday problems of life. They go struggling, even complaining, through their days with a sense of disappointment and discouragement feeling that life has, indeed, been stormy. J. Stuart Holden reminds us that "if we wait for ideally favorable weather for the sowing of the good seed, for the investment of our lives in the field of human need, we shall die waiting."

This book is written to suggest that we do not need to be defeated by anything, that we can find peace and happiness in a world filled with problems and frustrations. In short, our lives can be full of joy and satisfaction. An unidentified writer has rightly said:

> The way at times may dark and dreary seem.
> No ray of sunshine on our path may beam;
> The dark clouds hover o'er us like a pall,
> And gloom and sadness seems to compass all.
> But still with honest purpose toil we on.
> And if our steps be upright, straight, and true,
> Far in the east a golden light shall dawn,
> And the bright smile of God come bursting
>   through.

It is through the application of gospel principles that we can have that promise of sunshine.

This volume is not written under assignment of the Church, and the author alone is responsible for its ideas and contents.

As in times past I am most grateful to many for this work. I express particular appreciation to my wife, Jeanne, for her usual encouragement and unusual ability to help me put into writing what I feel and whose uncompromising standards of grammar and language keep her husband doing what earlier schoolteachers never could. A special thanks to my daughter Janet for editorial assistance and for her inspirational thoughts on "Morning" found in chapter 2, and to my daughter Marsha for her artistic ideas and suggestions for the dust jacket. Once again I express appreciation to my able secretary, Colleen Erickson, for her many hours of manuscript typing and attention to details. And thanks to David Christensen, a wonderful friend, for his ideas and many suggestions.

As always, I express deep gratitude to my daughters, Janet, Marsha, Kellie, and their families for being in my cheering section.

Decreasing Clouds: Trading Despair for Optimism

Variable Clouds, Occasional Rain, with a Promise of Sunshine

One who expects completely to escape low moods is asking the impossible. . . . Like the weather, [life] is essentially variable. . . . A healthy person believes in the validity of his high hours even when he is having a low one.'' (Harry Emerson Fosdick, *On Being a Real Person* [New York: Harper and Brothers, 1943], pp. 189, 193.)

Are you depressed? Or rather, have you ever been depressed? Now? Lately? Occasionally? Constantly?

Well, I honestly believe that although Dr. Fosdick was right and we will all suffer discouragement and depression, there is no reason to suffer needlessly. We can and should rise again—soon.

One thing I love about little people, our children, is their indomitable, positive spirits. They don't seem, generally, to be as bothered by depression as do adults, but appear to forever find the positive no matter how black the circumstances.

Speaking of those wonderful young men and women, I am reminded of the six-year-old son of an accountant for a large company. The little boy was used to hearing large sums of money mentioned at the dinner table and, not to be outdone, came racing into the house one Saturday and announced to his father that he'd just sold the family dog for ten thousand dollars.

"Sold the dog!" said the father. "What are you talking about? Where's the money?"

"Oh, I didn't get any money," said the boy. "It was a trade. I got two five-thousand-dollar cats for him."

There's no way to beat someone who won't be beaten. Six-year-olds are like that. Some young people and older adults have a harder time. At least I do, and I do not think I am alone. Someone once said, "There's a bright side to everything, but there's no joy when it's on the back of your blue suit."

I believe that there is a great difference between living in a world of discouragement and depression and being discouraged and depressed. It can be all around us but yet not *in* us. F. Scott Fitzgerald reminded us, "Trouble has no necessary connection with discouragement—discouragement has a germ of its own."

I like that thought. I like it because it's true. We all face problems and difficulties; however, we don't need to get depressed about it—at least, not for long. Ralph Waldo Emerson once stated, "Most of the shadows of life are caused by standing in our own sunshine." Problems and discouragement are not necessarily connected; that is, until we connect them.

Admitting that we have control of our emotions and feelings is a great first step. In fact, we may be our own worst enemies on that point. Our willing-ness to admit we are part of the problem is as necessary to the solution as knowing why we are discouraged or depressed. I admire those who have learned to come to that point. One of my heroes, Abraham Lincoln, was able to master this ability to assume responsibility for himself.

During the Civil War Lincoln, under severe political pressure, signed an order to transfer certain regiments from one field of battle to another. But Edwin M. Stanton, Lincoln's secretary of war, refused to carry out the orders, and said that Lincoln was a fool for having issued such an order.

The remark was passed on to Lincoln, who did not disagree: " 'If Stanton said I was a . . . fool then I must be one. For he is nearly always right, and generally says what he means. I will step over and see him.' " (Carl Sandburg, *Abraham Lincoln, The War Years*, vol. 2 [New York: Harcourt, Brace, and World, Inc., 1939], p. 62.)

Lincoln did just that and rescinded the order. Probably scores of spiritual lives could be saved if we would assume similar responsibility for decisions. And if we do that in one area we can do it in many. When we get discouraged and depressed, we can assume the responsibility for getting out—for we have the power to do just that.

Let me suggest another step which will help us on those days and occasions when we feel like we are going under for the third time. From my own experience I have found that much discouragement and depression come from giving in too soon.

A London physician, A. J. Cronin, because of poor health moved to a quiet farm in Scotland. There Cronin hoped to start a new career as a writer, a dream he had had since he was a lad.

For months he worked in a small attic room, filling notebook after notebook with handwritten text and sending it off to a London secretarial bureau to be typed. Finally the first typed chapters were returned in the mail. He picked them up eagerly, anxious to get a fresh impression of what he had written.

As Cronin read the manuscript, his disgust mounted. How could he have written such terrible material? He was a failure already, with his book only half-written. He stomped out into the drizzling rain for a lonely walk, throwing the manuscript into an ash pile beside the house.

Crossing the heath, he met a neighbor, an old farmer, digging a drainage ditch in a boggy field. The farmer inquired how Cronin's writing was coming along. When Cronin reported what he had done with his manuscript, the old farmer was silent for several minutes. Then he spoke.

"No doubt you're the one that's right and I am the one that's wrong. My father ditched this bog all his days and never made a pasture. But pasture or no pasture, I cannot help but dig. For my father knew, and I know, that if you only dig enough a pasture can be made here."

Ashamed of himself, Cronin walked back to the house, picked the manuscript up out of the ashes, and dried it out in the oven. Then he went back to work, writing and rewriting until it satisfied him. The book was *Hatter's Castle*, the first in a long string of successful novels.

What a tribute to a writer! And what a tribute to us when we do the same thing! Once again, "Trouble has no necessary connection with discouragement—discouragement has a germ of its own."

Theodore Roosevelt said, "It is hard to fail, but it is worse never to have tried to succeed." John Salak reminds us that "failures are divided into two classes—those who thought and never did, and those who did and never thought."

May I offer one bit of advice. I have found it useful

in my life. The principle comes from an account recorded in the Old Testament. Elisha, the prophet, had every reason to be depressed. He had successfully helped the king of Israel avoid the traps laid for him and his people by the king of Syria, but now Elisha was in deep trouble himself. The king of Syria had just arrived to take revenge:

"Therefore sent he thither horses, and chariots, and a great host: and they came by night, and compassed the city about.

"And when the servant of the man of God was risen early, and gone forth, behold, an host compassed the city both with horses and chariots. And his servant said unto him, Alas, my master! how shall we do?" (2 Kings 6:14–15.)

Elisha and a boy against the Syrian army! I think if I had been that boy I would not only have asked, "How shall we do?" but, in fact, would have asked several other questions, such as, "Are you sure we are doing the right thing?" or "Which way is the quickest exit?" But note:

"And he answered, Fear not: for they that be with us are more than they that be with them.

"And Elisha prayed, and said, Lord, I pray thee, open his eyes, that he may see. And the Lord opened the eyes of the young man; and he saw: and, behold, the mountain was full of horses and chariots of fire round about Elisha." (2 Kings 6:16–17.)

As you may recall, Elisha and the boy were victorious.

Now, I assure you that the same heavenly hosts are available to us in our day. They come to our rescue just as speedily as they did for Elisha and his servant. They can smite depression and despair. They can strike down discouragement and fear. They are available twenty-four hours a day, seven days a week. When we do all we can, when we have ex-

hausted all our resources, and when we humble ourselves and seek His help, it will be there. I know from
personal, sacred experiences that heavenly powers
can be released in our behalf. It has been true for me
and it is true for all. It is an eternally true principle.

I have not attempted to give a quick "how-to"
formula for overcoming depression, but I have
attempted to spell out some basic principles concerning our ability to win out in our battle against worry
and despair. As one man said, "You can't tell me
worry doesn't help. The things I worry about never
happen."

Well, we do worry, and we will get depressed, but
we don't have to stay that way. First, we can openly
admit we have it in our power to do something about
our depression and proceed to take the necessary
steps to change. Second, we can simply hang in there
and smile when the problem may not be of our own
making. This oft-quoted thought by Elbert Hubbard
gives us good counsel in handling both of these
points:

> God grant me the serenity to accept the
>   things I cannot change—
> The courage to change the things I can—
> And wisdom to know the difference.

And third, we can remember that there are hosts
from heaven who anxiously await the opportunity to
help when we are ready.

I know our lives will be filled with "variable cloud-
iness with a chance of some rain and snow," but I
also know that the sun will continue to shine. May
our eyes be open, just as Elisha's young friend had
his opened, with the added vision that there is no discouragement too great to handle and no depression
too severe to overcome.

2

Morning

Few things stir my emotions as much as a sunrise. It is one of God's greatest expressions of beauty. There have been times in my life, however, when I was not sure whether I would live to see the sun come up again. Those nights before the dawn were long.

How about you? Have you ever had the feeling that "I can't stand this another minute!" or "If I can just make it through the day!" Then, perhaps you also have wakened in the night and wondered if you would ever see the dawn of a new day. Those kinds of feelings are common to us all. Sometimes we may feel as if we are the only ones who have them, but I assure you it is not so. Who can live in this challenging world of ours and not have a few bumps and doubts along the way? Waking up in the middle of the night and worrying about one thing or another is part of being human.

Just remember, as surely as the sun sets, it rises

again . . . and again . . . and again, and with each new dawn comes a new start, a clean slate, and a chance for a new beginning. Thank goodness for a new day and an opportunity to forget yesterday. Every new day brings a fresh start, and every new morning brings new hope.

My daughter, Janet Gough, whose own life has demonstrated what a new day can bring, has caught the true significance of new beginnings in these words:

MORNING

MORNING BRINGS

Hope
Light
Faith
Confidence
Encouragement

MORNING DIMINISHES

Fear
Anxiety
Uncertainty
Unhappiness
Discouragement

MORNING ENHANCES

Eagerness
Excitement
Enthusiasm
Anticipation
Cheerfulness

MORNING INSPIRES

Desire
Capacity

Awareness
Intelligence
Determination

MORNING INVITES

Supplication
Repentance
Communication
Commitment
Achievement

MORNING MEANS

Awakening
Beginning
Renewing
Creating
Rejoicing

The Lord certainly knew what he was doing when he made twenty-four-hour days. That seems to be just the right amount of time to get some good things done, but not longer than we can bear when things are going wrong. My dad used to say, "The Lord certainly had his children in mind when he put a night between two days."

A great line in an old song says, "Nobody knows the trouble I've seen." Can you think of anyone who isn't experiencing trouble now or who will not have it in the future? Troubles come in all sizes, shapes, and kinds. But they do come! For some they may be physical or economic; for others they may be emotional or financial.

I am reminded of a research organization that was polling a small town to find out how the families spent their money. One old man told the young researcher that he spent 30 percent for shelter, 30 percent for clothes, 40 percent for food, and 20 percent for everything else. ''But that adds up to 120 percent,'' the young man protested.

''I know,'' said the old man, ''and it gets worse every year.''

I remember the good old days when it took a week to spend a week's wages. Those days are gone forever. The traditional family budget is now simply defined as ''a confirmation of your fears''!

Or our troubles may be job-related—bosses under pressure, unrealistic deadlines to meet, quotas to fill, and so on. They can be difficult, at best.

Then again, our troubles may be of a family nature —teenagers with problems, marriages in conflict, single parents trying to raise children, and on and on. I have a close friend who confides that he has four children—''two living and two teenagers.'' At least he has a sense of humor about it.

Then there are those struggles of a personal nature that we suffer alone. And even if those around us are aware of some of the problems, we still ''go it alone.'' These are private problems we all must work out by ourselves if we are to find any measure of happiness.

Even those are not all the kinds of problems we face, but they are some of the more obvious. A kind Heavenly Father gives us twenty-four-hour periods to handle them and then we begin anew. The sun goes down on the old, and it rises with a new promise of hope. With each new day there is comfort to be found. I believe that with all my heart.

Once again, I suggest that it was not accidental that the Lord made our days only twenty-four hours long. And I believe he intended that when one day ends, *we should let go of it.* How can we start a new day while we hold on to the old? Each day is a chance to begin again. It is, if you please, a rebirth. It can be if we will let it.

One of the most famous short stories ever written

is Guy de Maupassant's masterpiece "A Piece of String." The story's central figure is a Norman peasant by the name of Maitre Huchecorne. One day as he was walking through a busy marketplace, the frugal old peasant saw a bit of string lying on the ground. He stooped down and picked it up. Later he was accused of having picked up a wallet lost at that spot. He protested his innocence and exhibited the string, but he was arrested and taken to the police station. The next day the lost wallet was found, but Maitre was unable to forget his insult and began to brood over it. He told all his friends about the incident. Finally the piece of string became an obsession.

He neglected his farm to go about telling strangers how he had been mistreated and wrongly accused. Eventually the old peasant died of a broken heart. And in the delirium preceding his death, he was still mumbling something about a "piece of string."

What a tragedy! And, equally important, how unnecessary! The terms "end of a day" or "closing of a day" are exactly that. The day is to end, to close, to finish. When we lie down to rest, let's lay down the day at the same time. When eyes close, the day ends!

I'm a good one to give advice, my wife tells me. And as practical as this all sounds, if we're in the habit of continuing today into tomorrow, the habit is hard to break. On occasion, I am tempted to carry week into week and month into month.

Here is an example of this principle:

"The new family in the neighborhood overslept and the six-year-old daughter missed her school bus. The father, though late for work, agreed to drive her if she'd direct him.

"They rode several blocks before she told him to turn the first time, and several more before she indicated another turn. This went on for twenty minutes—yet when they finally reached the school, it proved to be only a short distance from their home.

"Asked why she'd led the father over such a circuitous route, the child explained, 'That's the way the school bus goes, and it's the only way I know.' "

Well, there is a better way! And that way is to learn to let go of each day and pick up the new one with hope. Forget the old—remember the new. I have a friend who tells me he used to be afraid of senility, but now that he's in it, he says it's really quite enjoyable. Forgetting is not all that bad when we forget what we need to.

There is one final thought about this twenty-four-hour period called "day." I find it symbolic that each day ends in darkness and begins in light. We can, if we want, lay each day down to rest. And as the sun rises, we can "resurrect" to a glorious new day. The darkness is left behind in the radiance of the sun. Light chases gloom away, and we are free to start clean and fresh. Yesterday is past; tomorrow is too far away to worry about. But while there is light, while there is today, we can start again. We can be happy.

As I mentioned earlier, there have been nights in my life so difficult to bear that I wondered if I could make it. But I did, and we all can! The night does end, the sun does rise again, and God does live.

May we put each day behind us and enthusiastically reach for the new. May we find comfort in Paul's testimony that "there hath no temptation taken you but such as is common to man: but God is faithful, who will not suffer you to be tempted above that ye are able; but will with the temptation also make a way to escape, that ye may be able to bear it" (1 Corinthians 10:13).

We can bear it! There is nothing so difficult that we cannot find our way out. It can be done with his help one day at a time. I know it to be so.

3

Start Over

A couple in California has started an interesting business. The two examine wills and locate missing heirs. When a will is filed and no heir comes forward to claim his share of the inheritance, the search begins and, like detectives, they piece together clues and bits of family history until they find the lucky benefactor.

On one such search the stakes were particularly high. It was a million-dollar inheritance. The couple searched records for months trying to find the heir, and finally their efforts paid off. The missing heir was a man being imprisoned in the Idaho State Penitentiary. They traveled to Idaho to tell him of his million-dollar prize, but when they arrived at the prison they didn't find him. His luck hadn't been so good after all. He'd escaped just a week earlier.

Sometimes getting the big prizes in life is just a matter of hanging on a little longer. It's a matter of not giving up even when you'd like to. Everybody starts out in life with big dreams; as children we have lain in the sunshine, have stared at the clouds, and have spun bright futures for ourselves. But one of life's hard rules is that obstacles come up on the way to achieving the something we set out to do. You know, you go to sail across the lake and your boat gets a hole in it. You meant to be on time but the phone rang just as you were leaving. You would have paid that bill but Michael lost the fluoride test and had to see the dentist. You would have been somebody but the position had already been filled.

Jesus Christ told his followers, ''Be ye therefore perfect, even as your Father which is in heaven is perfect'' (Matthew 5:48). But we who are walking through this minefield called mortality may wonder just what that means. If he'd only said, ''Be ye therefore adequate . . .'' or ''Be ye therefore just OK,'' we would have been fine. But so much is expected! How do we learn to control and master our physical environment—our homes, our debts, our dandelions—let alone our personal environment? How do we ever master our weaknesses, our selfishness, our impulse to yell ''uncle!''

One of the clues to learning self-mastery is that it is simply no crime to start over. Not one of us who is still breathing has arrived at that dreary day when we need to call ourselves failures. We may have been thrown from the horse a few times but we haven't failed, not as long as we are willing to stand up and try it again. Why are we so foolish as to think that when we are trying for something as difficult as self-mastery it can be done without practice? Why do we expect a polished performance on the first try out, or the second, or the forty-second? The grand prize in this case goes to those who are willing to start over and start over and start over again, every time getting just a little bit better. The prize goes to those who don't give up too easily even when giving up sounds sweet. Most of us try to master a weakness or character flaw and when we don't immediately succeed we publish and proclaim to the world that we can't do it. "Oh, I'm just hopeless," we say. "I'm just that way." "It'll never be different."

Let's not be so hard on ourselves! Progress for some of us may not even come line upon line. It may seem as we work with ourselves that it comes only dot upon dot. But isn't it worth it even if it comes that way?

Starting over! History reminds us that "Thomas Edison devoted ten years and all of his money to developing the nickel-alkaline storage battery at a time when he was almost penniless. Through that period of time, his record and film production were supporting the storage battery effort. Then one night the terrifying cry of fire echoed through the film plant. Spontaneous combustion had ignited some chemicals. Within moments all of the packing compounds, celluloids for records, film, and other flammable goods had gone up with a whoosh. Fire companies from eight towns arrived, but the heat was so intense and the water pressure so low that the fire hoses had no effect. Edison was sixty-seven years old—no age to begin anew. His daughter was frantic, wondering if he were safe, if his spirits were broken, how he would handle a crisis such as this at his age. She saw him running toward her. He spoke first. He said, 'Where's your mother? Go get her. Tell her to get her friends. They'll never see another fire like this as long as they live.' At 5:30 the next morning, with the fire barely under control, he called his employees together and announced, 'We're rebuilding.' One man was told to lease all the machine shops in the area, another to obtain a wrecking crane from the Erie

Railroad Company. Then, almost as an afterthought, he added, 'Oh, by the way, anybody know where we can get some money?'

"Virtually everything you now recognize as a Thomas Edison contribution to your life came *after* that disaster." (Jeffrey R. Holland, "For Times of Trouble," *New Era*, October 1980, p. 10.) Starting over? Aren't we glad Edison did?

And there's another sense in which starting over is an important concept in our lives. As long as we are growing, we are always starting over, picking up new skills, thrusting into new avenues of learning. The accomplished woman college student may suddenly find herself a very inept mother and homemaker. The accomplished doctor may find he knows nothing about putting in a garden. None of us are so knowledgeable and versatile that we are pros in all areas. We may be skilled in one area and a novice in another. At age seventy-five or eighty-five we will still be beginners at some things. Oliver Wendell Holmes started to study Greek just years before his death. The most exciting and vibrant people around us are smart enough to know that there are always some fields in which they are just beginning. They are willing to drop their stuffy stance of expertise and start over.

But there is one sense in which we had better be wary of starting over. It is best exemplified by the fellow who is an expert dieter—he's already been on twenty just this year. If we start over and start over, writing down the same resolutions again and again which never get reached, then it's time to take a new look at our lives. When we make no headway despite our keen desires, it is probably because starting over is not enough. We need to do something before we start over. We need to break some old patterns. There must be at least one pattern that we have each fallen into in our lives that is at best meaningless, and at worst harmful. Is it that we flip on the television every night at the same hour, forgetting how much we want to be well-read? Is it that we eat when we get under strain, forgetting in that moment how much we want to be thin? Is it that we get up at six-thirty, forgetting how much that extra half hour would mean to us if we could only get up at six? Examine your life and break some meaningless patterns before you start over. When you add something new to your life, it is usually done by taking something old away. Even the best organized among us have found that the closet only holds so much. Break some patterns, and then start over.

Today is a good day for starting over. That we may do so is my wish for us all.

4

Improve Your Situation

Does it ever seem as if everybody else gets all the luck? As one catchy tune suggests, "Some folks get cushions on their seat, center of the meat, houses on the street where it's sunny . . . and we get the rest." Success in life isn't really a question of luck —it's a matter of putting to work for yourself some key principles and seizing the opportunity when it comes your way.

In the days before we had modern harbors, ships had to anchor outside a port until a flood tide came to carry them in. As the time for the turning of the tide approached, skipper and crew took their places. As the tide reached its crest, all sprang into action. They knew that if they missed this tide, they would have to wait for another one and would lose the advantage of being first with their cargo in the market.

Shakespeare caught the meaning of "opportunity" in this passage:

There is a tide in the affairs of men,
Which, taken at the flood, leads on to fortune;
Omitted, all the voyage of their life
Is bound in shallows and in miseries.
(From *Julius Caesar.*)

If it seems to you that it is always the other person who has all the luck, if it seems that your life is bound up in the shallows while opportunities come in full flood to your neighbors, you may want to take note of these five basic principles for improving your situation:

1. Expect breaks to come your way.
2. Expose yourself to opportunities.
3. Be on the alert at all times.
4. Take the dare.
5. Follow through.

Let us see how each of these principles works.

First, expect breaks to come your way. Your opportunity really begins with you. Your attitude toward yourself will come as close to attracting luck or driving it away as any other single factor in your life. Do you believe in yourself? Do you expect opportunities to come your way? The winner of the race always knew he would be.

One child always said her prayers every night by thanking her Heavenly Father for her parents and grandparents and brothers and sisters, and then she ended them with, "Thank thee so much for me." That's how we all ought to feel—thankful for ourselves, full of belief in who we are and what we were meant to do.

An immigrant boy with hardly any English-speaking ability and with little schooling was sitting alone in Union Square with ten cents in his pocket.

He was debating whether he should spend the dime on a bowl of soup or buy five cents worth of peanuts and take the subway to the Bronx to apply for a job he had seen advertised. He had no friend to advise him and no prospects. The one thing he did have was a passionate belief that America is the land of opportunity.

He bought the peanuts, took the subway, and got the job. He began at a wage of $3.50 a week. It was modest but it was the chance at hand and he took it. Here was a stroke of good luck. His employer was a bachelor and later left to him the entire business because of his hard work.

Years later he was again sitting on the bench in Union Square when a bank vice-president spied him and walked over. "We have $140,000 worth of credit waiting for you in our bank any time you care to pick it up," he said.

The man who had been the boy debating about his total capital of ten cents smiled. By this time, he was the leading manufacturer in his field, the owner of one of the finest art collections in the world, and a great philanthropist honored by the libraries of famous universities. He had believed that in the land of opportunity there was an opportunity for him. He had expected it to come his way. When it came, he acted on it.

These breaks, of course, do not just come without some preparation, *so prepare yourself.*

"I will study and prepare myself and someday my chance will come," wrote young Abraham Lincoln. His came, and yours will too. Expect breaks to come your way.

The second key to improving your situation is to expose yourself to opportunities. "Behold, a sower went forth to sow" (Matthew 13:3). And the seeds which took root were those which made contact with fertile earth.

Don't let your friendships or your interests be narrow and confined. Read, study, listen to other people's ideas!

The third rule of success for improving your situation is to be on the alert for opportunities all the time. Look for opportunities to grow, to serve others, to improve yourself.

Two men were walking on the street when one of them stopped to pick up a five-dollar bill over which the other had just stepped.

"It's funny," said the second man, "but I have never found money on the street."

It was not funny. He never expected to find anything. He never learned to observe.

You can develop an eye for opportunity by the habit of always being on the lookout for it. Be observant. See what you look at. Hear what is said. Put two and two together in a different way. Be imaginative!

The fourth rule of success is to take the dare. You've heard the expression, "I'll buy that 'when my ship comes in.' " This expression has a story behind it. In the days of sailing ships, merchants would send out cargo loads of merchandise to be sold in the Orient. The money these cargos brought would then be spent to buy oriental silks, spices, and tea, with which the ships would sail back to their home ports. Every ship offered a double profit in this way but every ship also faced a double hazard—that of the storms which swept the seven seas and, even more threatening, that of the pirates who lay everywhere waiting to seize and plunder them.

Every ship sent out was a big gamble. All the merchants could do was to live sparsely at home and hope that the ships would come through. If they did, the merchants were sure to be wealthy men. Meanwhile, they would live on their plans of what to do when the ships came in. The important point for us here is this: No one can look forward to his ship coming in who has not first taken the dare of sending it out.

There comes a time when improving our situation demands that we take the dare. Send your ship out! The more ships you dare to send out, the more you dare to hope they will come through safely. Luck, as it is sometimes called, seldom settles on the man or woman who does not take the dare.

Abraham Lincoln signed the Emancipation Proclamation although his cabinet voted unanimously against him. He dared to do it.

I remember reading a story about a young man who saw an ad in the "help wanted" column of a Chicago newspaper. Instead of sending the usual reply letter the man sent a letter reading: "For the next twelve days I shall send you a postcard a day setting forth twelve reasons why you should hire me. On the thirteenth day I shall ask for an appointment." For twelve days he sent his postcards, numbered from one to twelve. On the thirteenth day he telephoned. The answer he heard was, "Come over at ten-thirty. We are all waiting to see what kind of a guy has been sending these cards." The young man, Glen Foushe, went on from there to become not only the owner of the company but also a popular national president of American Sales Executives Club.

If you want to improve your life, take the dare.

And the last rule for success is the big one: Follow through. Part of the price of improving is to have the patience and persistence to carry your plan to attainment. Remember, innovations are seldom welcomed with enthusiasm when they are first introduced. Everybody is suspicious of that which is new and different.

Westinghouse was practically thrown out of the railroad offices when he came along with his new brake. He was told that the brakes in use did the job well enough.

Alexander Graham Bell peddled his telephone literally all over the East before he found enough investors to launch a company.

There are still people living who can remember the mocking cry, "Hire a horse," shouted at unhappy pioneer automobilists whose cars broke down beside the road.

You were meant to succeed. Just remember the five principles when you are beginning to feel that everybody else has all the luck. Expect the opportunities to come your way. Expose yourself to those opportunities. Be on the lookout all the time. Take the dare. Follow through.

And if you will, I promise you joy and success in all you do.

5

Cans and Can'ts

People are amazing! They can do impossible things when they make up their minds to do so. Age has nothing to do with it; neither does race, creed, or economic status. And sometimes the "impossible" acts can be quite dramatic. Some years ago I read of a remarkable incident from the life of a remarkable woman:

"May Haviland was a middle-aged Quaker with a ramrod bearing and the softest brown eyes in the world. Quaker ancestors had suffered persecution in early America rather than compromise their principles. One of them was nonresistance and it was bred into May Haviland's bones.

"The Havilands were a well-to-do old family, and May was the last of a long line of them. She lived unostentatiously in Brooklyn but made at least one trip abroad every year. Paris was her favorite destination and she stayed always at the same modest pension [hotel], where her habits were like clockwork. It was well known, too, that she brought with her the family jewels inherited from a succession of aunts and cousins.

"One evening she came down to dinner intending to spend her usual hour or two in the lobby reading newspapers. But this night she discovered that she had forgotten her handkerchief, so after the meal she went back to her room for it.

"As May opened her door, she was astounded to see a burly, dark-haired man rifling her bureau drawers. Quietly May closed the door behind her and at the faint click the burglar whirled, a revolver in his hand.

" 'If there's one thing I dislike,' she told the intruder firmly, 'it's guns. Please put that thing down. I am not going to call for the police. I am going to help you because you must need whatever I have much more than I do, if you have to steal for it.'

"The burglar was utterly dumbfounded when May opened the secret drawer of a small rosewood desk where her rings were hidden. She talked to him quietly, reassuringly, pressing the jewelry on him and telling him that she was sorry for him since his need was so urgent.

"Suddenly the man dropped his gun to the floor, let out a low cry and fled, taking nothing." (*Guideposts*, November 1961.)

Not bad for a senior citizen. In fact, that wasn't bad for any age. Apparently at some time in her life, May Haviland learned one of life's great secrets. I'm not sure who said it, but whoever did really understands life: "Success comes in cans, failure in can'ts."

Henry Ford put it this way: "Whether you think you can or whether you think you can't, you're right." May Haviland evidently thought she could take an improbable approach to an impossible situation and make something positive happen. And she did.

I watched with great interest this season as the greats of the NBA competed in a "slam-dunk" contest on national television. There were gathered some of the greatest basketball players in the history of the game. Their abilities were amazing to behold. Watching them was a pleasure. I was especially fascinated to see the winner of the contest. In an era of seven-foot centers, the slam-dunk contest was won by the smallest basketball player in the NBA, "Spud" Webb of the Atlanta Hawks. He stands only five feet, seven inches tall and he was declared the best of the "jammers." Evidently no one told the "Spud" that he had no chance against the bigger boys of the league. Have you ever seen a pint-sized, five-foot-seven-inch ball of fire float through the air and slam a basketball through the hoop? Spud Webb comes in a can, not a can't!

I always enjoy humor. I especially enjoy it when it is sprinkled with truth. In light of May Haviland and Spud Webb and others like them, consider the following:

1. A famous English scientist wrote a book proving that steamboats could never cross the Atlantic. The first copy brought to America came over on a steamboat.

2. When rayon was first put on the market, a committee appointed by the silk manufacturers to study its possibilities declared it a "temporary fad."

3. Joshua Coppersmith was arrested in Boston for trying to sell telephone stock. "All well-informed people know that it is impossible to transmit the human voice over a wire," he was told.

4. In 1811 when the New York YMCA announced typing lessons for women, vigorous protests were made on the grounds that the female constitution would break down under the strain.

5. In Germany, it was proved by experts that if trains went at the frightful speed of fifteen miles per hour, blood would spurt from the travelers' noses and that passengers would suffocate going through tunnels.

6. The first successful cast-iron plow, invented in the United States in 1797, was rejected by New Jersey farmers under the theory that cast iron poisoned the land and stimulated the growth of weeds.

7. Chauncey M. Depew confessed that he warned his nephew not to invest five thousand dollars in Ford stocks because "nothing has come along to beat the horse."

8. When patents were taken out for the steel-frame skyscraper in 1888, the *Architectural News* predicted that the expansion and contraction of iron would crack all the plaster, eventually leaving only the shell.

And now for the classic:

9. The bumblebee cannot fly. According to the theory of aerodynamics, and as may be readily demonstrated through laboratory tests and wind-tunnel experiments, the bumblebee is unable to fly. This is because the size, weight, and shape of his body in relation to the total wingspread makes flying impossible. But the bumblebee, being ignorant of these scientific truths, goes ahead and flies anyway— and makes a little honey every day.

Now, that's my kind of list—can'ts that became cans!

I have always taught that thinking you can do

something is getting at least half of the task done already. I believe all great men and women, including teenagers and children, understand what Winston Churchill once taught:

"At one time . . . Churchill went back to the old school where he had studied as a boy and where he carved his initials in the benches as they do in Britain. The headmaster told the boys, 'The greatest man, the greatest Britisher, of our time is going to come to this school and I want you all to be here with your note-books; I want you to get down what he says because his speech will be something for you to remember all your lives.'

"So the old man came. They introduced him. He stood there, looking down at the boys. He had his glasses like he used to have—down on the end of his nose. And then he delivered words from an immortal speech he once gave to Parliament. He said: 'Never! Never! Never give up!' And with that, he sat down. That was the speech. It was immortal; something to be remembered forever by every boy who heard him.''

Such an attitude will take us a long way. I often contrast that with a statement I hear from time to time. The words may vary but it always goes some-thing like this: "You know, I've half a mind to do something about that," or, "I have half a mind to try that." Then, of course, nothing gets done. Perhaps a more accurate phrasing would be "I've half a mind." Period! Having "half a mind" makes a very small mind indeed. Little minds do the do-able; great minds do the undo-able.

Some years ago there appeared an article written by Hugh Price Hughes titled "Ubique." This is the Latin word for *everything*, and the story was intended to be a satire on professed Christians.

The gist of it was that a man had occasion to go for the first time to the town of Ubique on business. He arrived at the railroad station on a blustery December day. There was a cold wind and a flurry of snow. As he walked along the street he saw women dressed in costly furs and gentlemen in fur coats, but all had bare feet. The population seemed respectable and well-to-do, but no one wore shoes. They limped along, afflicted with chilblains and bruises and suffering great pain.

When he went to the hotel he found the desk clerk, the bellboys, and other attendants all barefoot. At the dinner table he sat next to a prosperous-looking old gentleman and fell into conversation. As this new acquaintance seemed so kindly and open-minded, our traveler said to him, "Pardon me if I seem intrusive, but I notice that nobody in this town seems to wear shoes, yet everyone appears to suffer from cold and bruised feet. Would you mind telling me why?"

"Ah," said the old gentleman, raising his eyes piously. "Why indeed!"

The visitor talked further with his companion but could never get past that point. The old gentleman was perfectly willing to admit that shoes were desirable above all things and that everybody ought to wear them, but he could not tell why they did not do so.

The traveler took a walk through the town and found that here and there were beautiful buildings, more elaborate and larger than the ordinary. Seeing the janitor sweeping the steps of one of these structures, he stopped and talked to him.

"What is this building? I am a stranger in the town and notice there are many buildings like this."

"This is a shoe factory," said the janitor.

"Oh, then they make shoes here?"

"Oh, not at all," was the reply. "They just talk about making shoes."

I guess talk is, after all, fairly cheap.

Well, where do we fit? Are we really capable of doing the impossible? My answer is a resounding "Yes, we can!"

Let's start with the tasks at hand. What have we already been called to do? Raise a family? Change our jobs? Fill a difficult assignment? Clean our room? Make it through school?

I remember a story of a disheartened craftsman who had been serving in a community for some time with seemingly few results:

"One night he had a dream in which he was trying to break a large granite rock with a pickax. Hour after hour he labored but with no results. At last he said, 'It's no use. I'm going to quit.' Suddenly a man appeared by his side and asked, 'Were you not appointed to this task? And if so, why are you going to abandon it?' 'My work is in vain,' said the artist. 'I can make no impression on the granite.' 'That is not your concern; your duty is to keep at it,' replied the stranger. 'The work is yours, the results are in another's hands; work on!' In his dream, the man saw himself taking the ax in hand again, and at his first blow, the granite flew into hundreds of pieces."

An unidentified author has reminded us:

Stick to your task till it sticks to you;
Beginners are many, but enders are few.
Honor, power, place, and praise
Will come, in time, to the one who stays.
Stick to your task till it sticks to you.
Bend at it, sweat at it, smile at it too.

For out of the bend and the sweat and the smile
Will come life's victories, after a while.

Again I ask, "What is our task?" Whatever it is, we can do it magnificently! We can do it even if it seems undo-able. The secret is to keep at it, and at it, and at it. It can be done. And there is power available above and beyond our own. I have experienced it; so have you. When we're at our task, when we righteously persist, a kind Heavenly Father will push us over the top. He will help us to be victorious. If the task is righteous and we have done all we can do, he will make up the difference. What this world needs is more "cans" and less "can'ts." May we all become "can-do's."

6

I Am What
I Am

Someone asked a famous conductor of a great symphony orchestra which orchestral instrument he considered the most difficult to play. The conductor thought for a moment, and said: 'Second fiddle. I can get plenty of first violinists. But to find one who can play second fiddle with enthusiasm— that's a problem. And if we have no second fiddles, we have no harmony.' ''

Whoever that conductor was certainly knew people, and ever since I heard that little incident, I have contemplated its implications in many areas besides music. I have a friend who plays the violin very well. I asked him if violinists are really that way. His answer was affirmative. I suppose I really shouldn't have had to ask. I guess all of us want to play first violin, be first team or first vice-president. But I have watched sports long enough to know that a sixth man coming off the bench in basketball can be as valuable as a starter; a teller at the bank can do as much good as the head cashier; a pink lady at the hospital can contribute just as much, even if she isn't the head nurse.

And so it is. We can't all be the best in everything, but we can be our best in whatever we do. It may not be sitting in the first chair of the orchestra, or being named a football all-American, but we can make our own contribution to the harmony of mankind. What we need more of in this world are good second fiddles . . . I say again, not just second fiddles, but good ones.

Do you remember a young man in Old Testament times named Enoch? When the Lord called him to be of service, he responded as would many of us. His reply was a classic: "I . . . am but a lad, and all the people hate me; for I am slow of speech" (Moses 6:31).

Isn't that interesting? Here was a member of the team who hadn't yet really suited up, but when he did he not only played on the team, he became an assistant coach. He started with what he was and went from there. He took his whole city to heaven— however, not in a day.

I think the key to playing a great second violin, and to almost anything else we do, is to feel our own worth and value. It's to understand who we really are and what we are.

I have a very good friend, Frank Day, who has taught school for many years. I suppose he has influenced thousands of young men and women over his lifetime. He tells a remarkable story of one of his students:

"One day he walked into our religion class somewhat frightened, maybe a little belligerent, certainly not at ease. Few spoke to him; no one walked with him. He had almost no friends.

"For one so young his life had been a most difficult one. His father had been killed in a drunken
brawl; his mother was not interested in sending them
[her children] to school. She was on state welfare,
and much of that money was used to purchase liquor
for herself and her boyfriends.

"Even the most basic material goods were lacking
in the home, including adequate food and clothing.
The boy had only a sweater to keep him warm in the
cold weather. As he walked to school, he would take
the sweater off as he approached the building,
because it had large holes in it and he didn't want his
peers to see. (I say peers because he had no friends.)
He wore no socks because he had none. His hands
were rough and chapped because the house had only
cold water and no soap with which to wash. This boy
was thin and lacked vitality. Food was not plentiful,
and that available was of the junk food variety. He
lived in an unkempt area on the far side of town and
was uncomfortable when he visited any other section
of the community.

"The first day of class I invited him to sit on the
front row. He did so willingly but not comfortably. I
tried to make friends with him, but it was very difficult. He appeared to trust no one.

"After school had been in session for several
weeks, I asked if he would like to give the prayer. He
quickly and emphatically refused. I later learned that
he had never heard a prayer until his first day in that
class. He had never been to church. As the days
passed there was little change in his willingness to
communicate, to smile, or to seek friends.

"A month before the Christmas holidays, one
young lady requested class time to present a matter of
concern. The young man was absent that day, and as
she stood before the group her message was simply:

'We are not friendly with him, we do not speak with him, we do not walk with him, we do not associate with him. This seems to me to be very wrong. After all, he is important too.' Then she suggested that they could and should be friendly to him and help him to understand how important he was—his importance to them and to himself. They all agreed to respond to her recommendations. Then she suggested that they each contribute a small amount of money toward buying him a coat for Christmas. This they also willingly accepted.

"One did not have to be told that they were succeeding. It was in his eyes, in his walk, and in his smile. It was obvious to everyone that there was a change in his life. He walked a little taller. He was able to look others in the eye and smile as he extended a friendly greeting.

"One day there was a note on the teacher's desk which read, 'If you cannot find someone to give the prayer today, I will,' and he signed his name. Strangely enough no one would give the prayer that day, so I called on him. He did not close his eyes. He did not fold his arms. He did not bow his head or do any of the things we normally do in prayer. He simply looked up to the ceiling with his hands by his side and said, "Oh, God, help us. Amen." No one smiled. No one coughed. No one said a word. It was a wonderful prayer to him and to every member of the class.

"Two or three days before the Christmas vacation, the young lady who had proposed the plan came to class with a beautifully wrapped Christmas package and again requested class time. She stood and thanked each of the students for their kindness and their willingness to respond to her earlier suggestions. Then she spoke for just a moment about the value of individuals regardless of their status in life, their home background, their scholastic abilities, or their popularity. She said that everyone is important. The young man, a bit suspicious at first, suddenly became aware the young lady was about to involve him in a new experience.

"After some moments, she took him by the arm and had him stand by her side. She told him how much they appreciated him and how valuable he was to the class. She said they all appreciated him and were pleased he was their friend. By now he had tears in his eyes, but so did the teacher and most of the class. She then laid the package in his arms, and the tears increased. After a moment or two passed, another young man in the class said, 'If you will open the package you can see what's in it.'

"Slowly, methodically, with great care and a desire not to tear the paper, he opened the package and held up a beautiful jacket. He continued to display his emotions, and so did the class. After some moments the same boy said, 'If you'll unzip it you can put it on.' He opened the zipper and slowly put his arms into each sleeve, pulling the jacket around him and displaying a happy smile through the tears. He wore the coat every day until the last week in May."

Can you guess what happened to that young man? You're right! He married well, is raising a great family, and in addition, his mother and brothers and sisters were all changed. He didn't become the president of a bank or the chairman of a board of directors, but he became one of the best second fiddles around—temporarily. With the new direction he had gained, who's to say where his natural potential will take him!

That brings me to one final point. Lest you and I forget what orchestras and teams are all about, just remember that the Apostle Paul had some problems of his own. He not only wasn't a member of the team, but he tried to throw the game before it started. In fact, he tried to do away with some of the players. Fortunately, he repented and began a long and glorious career as a servant of the Lord. As he once reflected on his past, and on his own inadequacies, he made a comment of eternal worth, ''But by the grace of God I am what I am: and his grace which was bestowed upon me was not in vain'' (1 Corinthians 15:10).

There it is: ''I am what I am.'' Once we learn who we really are—our talents and limitations—and accept ourselves even with all our frailties, we can be the best that we can be. Some of us will play first violin; some will play second fiddle, but we will all be a part of the team and we will contribute. Then, Paul's second statement will be absolutely true: ''And his grace which was bestowed upon me was not in vain.''

You and I, all of us, have talents. Some are earned and many are God-given. They are to bless us and those around us. Some have great talent, some have less, but all have some. We can all contribute. A kind, wise Heavenly Father expects us to do so. We are his children and he is our leader. Thank God for great parking lot attendants, store clerks, gas station mechanics, postal clerks, and a million others who supposedly play second fiddle. And thank God for great neurosurgeons, bank presidents, attorneys, astronauts, and a million others who supposedly sit in the first chair. But I particularly thank God for us, his children, who have come to know who and what we are and how to use our talents for the benefit of all mankind.

One final thought: I really believe that in the life to come we can all occupy the first chair. A wise Father's criterion for success is not based on which chair we sit in or which position we happen to hold, but on the effort we are willing to put forth in that chair or position.

7

Be Proud of
Your Spots

One thing my grandchildren do for me is motivate me to read. I admit that the reading material is not always on subjects I would choose, but, then again, there aren't a lot of children's stories on golf or baseball.

However, the other day I did read a verse which was not only clever but very profound. I doubt if some of my grandchildren really got the full meaning; however, it is well worth repeating to any adult audience. It stated:

A leopard named Bella cried, "Shivering tots!
There's something the matter with me.
My young sister Bessie has fifty-four spots,
But I only have fifty-three!"

Just to make sure, Bella counted some more,
Hoping her sister had less,
But the count of her sister's remained fifty-four—
One extra spot for young Bess.

Bella cried, "Fie! Oh, fiddledeedee!"
And ran through the jungle to hide.
She climbed to the top of a coconut tree,
Where she helplessly broke down and cried.

She wept a whole bucket of splattery tears
For at least seven-eighths of an hour.
Then along came a monkey who said, "Fan my ears!
I do think it's starting to shower!"

The little brown monkey grumbled and sighed,
And hoisted his purple umbrella.
Then up in the treetop he suddenly spied
The blubbering, bellowing Bella.

"I say there!" he shouted, "Now just cut that out,
You're a bit of a nuisance, my pet.
If you don't stop that crying there isn't a doubt
That somebody's going to get wet!"

"Have pity!" sobbed Bella, "I'm tied up in knots,
And my heart is as sore as a blister.
I discovered I only have fifty-three spots,
And there're fifty-four spots on my sister!"

Then the monkey sat down 'neath the coconut tree,
And laughed with a rollicking rumble.
He held his fat sides as he chuckled with glee,
Then he fell on his back with a tumble.

"Thank goodness!" he laughed, "that there're no
        two the same
Under the sun and the moon.
Were I like my cousins, 'twould sure be a shame,
For my cousin's an ugly baboon!"

Then Bella climbed down from the lofty treetop
And happily started to purr.
Using her pink leopard tongue for a mop,
She washed the brown spots on her fur.

"Fifty-three—fifty-four—a spot less or more,
What does it matter?" laughed she.
"At least I can always be certain and sure
That there's no one exactly like me!"
        (Francis B. Watts, "Bella's Spots," *Friend*,
        June 1978, pp. 20–21.)

Isn't that true? We may all have spots, but no two of us are alike and that is a great blessing. We are all unique and different; however, I sometimes smile when I think what happens when we don't always understand that great truth.

A story is told of a motorcyclist who on a wintry night reversed his jacket so that the bitter winds would not come through the gaps between the buttons. The jacket was somewhat uncomfortable, back-to-front, but it served the purpose. As he sped along the road, he skidded on an icy spot and the poor fellow crashed into a tree.

When the ambulance arrived, the paramedics pushed through the crowd and asked the person who was standing over the victim what had happened. The man replied that the motorcyclist seemed to be in pretty good shape after the crash, but by the time they got his head straightened out, he was dead.

So it goes when we get excited about spots or events without fully comprehending. In the long run, we are better off if we accept our situations for what they are and appreciate our differences.

In the course of my life, I have had the privilege of being involved with many people. I have listened to countless numbers as they have poured out their frustration at being who they are. Their self-esteem is often low. Their lack of self-worth is continually dragging them down. I suppose that if I had enjoyed only that experience with so many of my fellowmen, my attitude would be anything but positive. But I am happy to report that I try to be positive, and one of the reasons I do is because I have witnessed so many of these friends as they have come to realize their worth. What a difference that makes!

George Durrant, a wonderful friend, learned to like himself early in his childhood. He has been kind enough to put into words an experience that changed his life. I share his insight in his own words:

"I was in the ninth grade. A year in which it seemed I was halfway to nowhere. Confidence was not part of my nature. My actions were largely controlled by my feelings of inferiority.

"During third period I sat near the back of the classroom. My feet extended as far forward as I could stretch them. By sitting in this manner I was scarcely visible from where the teacher sat at her desk in the front.

"Friday was the day for current events. When the roll was called, each student had two choices—he could either answer 'prepared' or 'unprepared.' If his response was 'unprepared' he didn't have to do anything. I quickly grasped the idea that the word 'unprepared' was the word that would get me off the hook.

"As the weeks went by, each time my name was called I responded almost with dignity, 'Unprepared.' My friends also mastered this word. We all, as a group, made it easier for each of us as individuals.

"A girl that I liked very much sat in front of me. I liked her so much that on the way to school I would think of clever things to say to her, but when in her presence, my mind would go blank and I would become almost tongue-tied.

"One day when the teacher called the roll and got to my name, I replied, 'Unprepared.' It was then that this girl did me a great favor. She turned around, looked back at me, and said, 'Why don't you get prepared?' I was not able to listen to any of the reports that day. I kept thinking of all sorts of wonderful things like, 'What does she care, unless she cares?'

"I went home, found an article in the newspaper, and read it time and again until I had finally committed it to memory. I cut the article out, folded it, placed it in my wallet, and carried it with me all week.

"The next Friday I was there in my usual seat in the back. The teacher started to call the roll without looking up. Finally she got to my name; she said 'George?' and very quietly I gave a great speech—I said, 'Prepared.'

"She stopped calling the roll and looked up at me. I poked my head up as far as I could and nodded. The girl turned around and smiled. My friends looked over at me like, 'Traitor!' Then I sat waiting my turn, saying to myself, 'What have I done?' I was scared. Then I made a magnificent discovery. It was all right to be afraid if I didn't let it stop me from doing what I should.

"My turn came. I went to the front and started to speak. I remembered every word, and after the last word had crossed my lips, I stood there for just a second, and a priceless thought passed my mind and found its way to my heart. I said to myself, 'I like you!'

"I returned to my seat and sat down. I didn't hear any of the reports, but as my heart pounded within me, I kept feeling over and over again, 'This is the only way to live.'

"I have since learned that the word 'unprepared'

really does take you off the hook and lead you away from pressure. By learning to say that word you really don't have to do anything, but you never know the joy of doing something that causes you to say to yourself, 'I like myself.' " (George Durrant, "Halfway to Nowhere," *New Era*, Jan.-Feb., 1981, p. 39.)

Wouldn't it be great if all children could have such an experience? Unfortunately, many young people do not get close to that and by the time they're teenagers, their low self-esteem can be a very real problem—to parents and to themselves.

That leads me to another point. Since developing a good self-image begins early in childhood, I suggest that a concentrated effort by parents can make a difference in how our children and youth see themselves—an eternal difference. We need to point out their virtues at every opportunity. How about some starters:

1. "You know one of the things I like about you? You're fun to be around."

2. "You have a great smile."

3. "I'm sure proud of your attitude."

4. "You look wonderful today."

5. "We're sure glad you're ours."

And the list goes on. Simple but sincere compliments can transform children into something great— which is exactly what they are! Can you imagine how teenagers would respond to such treatment? And how about parents, grandparents, or friends?

May I say once again that I have seen lives change as men and women discover for themselves that fifty-three spots are as good as fifty-four; ten are as good as ninety. We are all children of the same Father. He loves even those without spots.

Let us consider the message and dedicate ourselves to lifting those around us to new heights of self-esteem.

Greater Visibility: Seeking for Personal Perfection

On My Honor

Recently I had a special thrill as I sat in a Boy Scout Court of Honor. Following a very impressive and somewhat emotional ceremony, a young man with a gentle but firm demeanor stood with his right arm to the square giving the Scout sign. As he did so with great pride and dignity, he uttered these words: "On my honor I will do my best to do my duty to God and my country . . ." (Scout Oath).

When a boy stands and pledges that on his honor he will do his best to do his duty to God and his country, he is in a position to learn one of the fundamental lessons in life.

There is no happiness without honor; there is little success without doing one's best. What are we without good character? And can good character exist without honor? When we look at the life and teachings of the Savior, it was the hypocrite who received his criticism; it was the honesty of the widow who gave her mite which has lived in our memories ever since. Judas will forever be an example of dishonor, while the prayer in Gethsemane will always be the standard of true devotion. What better attribute can a boy learn than honor?

I think it is wonderful and exciting to be around people who are responsible—who take full responsibility for their lives and actions. And yet I am sure we have all been around those who take every opportunity to blame other people or events for their difficulties. To put it bluntly, they can be a real trial. They are often the ones who find excuses or tell "white lies" in order to shift the responsibility. I remember reading once of a collection of such "American fibs." I think many will sound familiar to you. Have you ever heard:

—The check is in the mail.
—I'll start my diet tomorrow.
—We always service what we sell.
—Give me your number and the doctor will call you right back.
—Money is cheerfully refunded.
—One size fits all.
—This offer is limited to the first one hundred people who call in.
—Your luggage isn't lost, it's only misplaced.
—Leave your resume and we'll keep it on file.
—This hurts me more than it hurts you.
—I just need five minutes of your time.
—Your table will be ready in a few minutes.
—Open wide—it won't hurt a bit.
—Let's have lunch sometime.
—It's not the money, it's the principle.

The list has no end and, while we can't help but smile when we hear such statements, we all know better. I suppose it is only natural that we try to defend our image or pride by making such claims.

But in reality, we can only go so far. There comes a time when we all must not only recognize our deceptive ways but also be willing to make the change.

Aesop, in his marvelous fables, puts things into proper perspective. In his parable "The Lark and Her Young Ones," he says:

"A lark made her nest in a field of young wheat. As the days passed, the wheat stalks grew tall and the young birds also grew in strength. Then one day, when the ripe golden grain waved in the breeze, the farmer and his son came into the field.

" 'This wheat is now ready for reaping,' said the farmer. 'We must call in our neighbors and friends to help us harvest it.'

"The young larks in their nest close by were much frightened, for they knew they would be in great danger if they did not leave the nest before the reapers came. When the mother lark returned with food for them, they told her what they had heard.

" 'Do not be frightened, children,' said the mother lark. 'If the farmer said he would call in his neighbors and friends to help do his work, this wheat will not be reaped for a while yet.'

"A few days later, the wheat was so ripe that when the wind shook the stalks, a hail of wheat grains came rustling down on the young larks' heads."

" 'If this wheat is not harvested at once,' said the farmer, 'we shall lose half the crop. We cannot wait any longer for help from our friends. Tomorrow, we must set to work ourselves.'

"When the young larks told their mother what they had heard that day she said: 'Then we must be off at once. When a man decides to do his own work and not depend on someone else, then you may be sure there will be no more delay.'

"There was much fluttering and trying out of wings that afternoon. At sunrise next day, when the farmer and his son cut down the grain, they found an empty nest. Self-help is the best help."

I have long felt that that fable teaches a marvelous lesson. We can only wait so long to take action. But when a person finally makes up his mind to be responsible for his own life and destiny, watch out!

One of the great books in the Old Testament is the account of Esther and her love for her people. Esther was a beautiful Jewish girl. She was selected by the king of Persia to be his queen. However, there was a slight problem. The king did not know she was Jewish. Then, because of Haman, the king's minister, a royal decree went out calling for the execution of all the Jews in the kingdom.

One of the laws of the kingdom stipulated that no one could enter the king's inner court without his personal invitation. The penalty for violation of that command was death—"except such to whom the king shall hold out the golden sceptre" (Esther 4:11).

Esther had not been in the presence of the king for thirty days, but with the situation as serious as it was, she took action. With the lives of her people at stake, she decided to go to the king himself, knowing the potential disaster that awaited her. Her words are an eternal testimony of one young woman and her willingness to assume responsibility for herself. She said, "And if I perish, I perish" (Esther 4:16).

What a great statement! "And if I perish, I perish." In other words, "Let the chips fall where they may. I will do the right thing and I'll take full responsibility." Esther knew all about the Scout Oath long before it was articulated by Baden-Powell.

Robert E. Lee, one of America's most illustrious and dedicated pioneers, puts it another way: "Duty is the sublimest word in our language. Do your duty in all things. You cannot do more. You should never wish to do less.'' (John Bartlett, *Bartlett's Familiar Quotations*, 14th ed. [Boston: Little, Brown and Company, 1968], p. 620.) That's real responsibility! An associate of mine often says it another way, ''All you can do is all you can do.''

I have always been interested in watching what happens in another's life when it comes time to take responsibility. All of us are called on to make difficult decisions at times—adults and children alike. Have you ever noticed that even children's little minds struggle just like our big minds? I suppose that, regardless of age, we all have the urge to rationalize, even a little. As an example:

''A story is told of a woman who had been shopping and had bought a dress that she knew she could not afford. 'Why did you do it?' Her husband asked.

'' 'I just couldn't help it,' she alibied. 'The devil tempted me.'

'' 'Why didn't you say, ''Get thee behind me, Satan''?' the husband asked.

'' 'I did, but he just leaned over my shoulder and whispered, ''My dear, it fits you beautifully in the back.'' ' ''

Most husbands could understand that comment.

Realizing our own need to be responsible for our actions can be painful. It can be quite difficult, but it is most rewarding. As I visit the Church and elsewhere I continue to find thousands of Esthers and Robert E. Lees who have not only assumed their responsibilities but who also enjoy the challenge.

If you have yet to start to take hold of your own life, why don't you begin with the small things— taking out the trash, making beds, doing dishes, paying the bills; then move forward to greater challenges—being virtuous, honest, and being concerned about important issues. I believe it can be done. May we understand that one of our greatest responsibilities is to be responsible. And may it be our lot to find the real joy that comes from our own pledge to do our very best for our God, country, and all else that may confront us.

9

To Tell the Truth

I cross my heart and hope to die." When I was much younger my friends and I used to make that pledge. That's what we used to say to convince each other that we were telling the truth. In ancient Palestine the people had a different custom. When one was anxious to prove his honesty, he said to another, "I swear by heaven that I speak the truth," or "by the hair of my head," or by any number of things that were held especially sacred. The Savior himself, seeing this custom and realizing how fruitless its use was in building a successful life, said that the thing to do was not to prove our honesty by oaths, but to be so truthful that oaths would not be necessary to substantiate our word. "Let your communication be, Yea, yea; Nay, nay," he said (Matthew 5:37). Be so truthful and so above suspicion in all that you speak or do that when you say "yes" people know that "yes" is right, and when you say "no" they can be assured that "no" is correct.

Recently I had to smile while talking with a friend. After a period of conversation he looked at me, lowered his voice, and said, "Paul, to tell the truth . . ." Then he finished his comment. If he was now telling me the truth, I wondered what he had been telling me up to that point.

Truth can have a humorous side. I remember seeing a bumper sticker which read, "You're ugly and your mother dresses you funny." It could be more discreetly stated, but I suppose there was an element of truth there for some.

The principle of truth is often funny, sometimes serious, occasionally deadly, but it is always real and every generation must learn it. Some do better than others, but to be really happy with ourselves and with life we must come to grips with truth. It is all around us. It is what it is. Shakespeare said, "Is not the truth the truth?" (*King Henry the Fourth, Part I.*)

Coming to grips with a definition of truth has always been a challenge for the philosophers of this world. When Christ was arraigned before Pilate, the Roman procurator asked his now-famous question, "What is truth?" (John 18:38). Christ taught him a principle concerning truth, for Pilate never found it on his own. For our purpose here, no definition is really needed. The honest in heart recognize truth wherever they find it.

There are, however, some critical things to be said about truth. First, as Mark Twain said, "Truth is the most valuable thing we have." If we can just learn to treasure truth, we'll have found one of life's great secrets—as we come to value truth, we will be true to it. When we do that, we'll be loyal to the truth within us, even if, sometimes, it means forgoing or giving up that which might seem very desirous at the time, but which would ultimately bring only temporary satisfaction. Such was the case of a young man who was true to his innermost feelings:

"Two young medical students at the University of Michigan had just finished their classes one day in the spring of 1883. It was a time of great hope and anticipation for them; in a few weeks they would receive their medical degrees. All the hard work, the long hours would soon be rewarded—they would be doctors.

"They were relaxing now in their rooms and their thoughts naturally reverted to what they would do with their lives. The two were as different in outward appearance as two men could be: the one short, stocky; the other tall, thin, with blue eyes.

" 'Come on, Will,' the short, stocky one was saying, 'come to New York with me. We'll be rich in no time at all. What do you say?'

"It was obvious that their conversation was a continuation of discussions they had been having for several months now—centering around the dream of going east and setting up a partnership in New York City.

" 'I'm sorry, Ben,' the other young man replied, 'but the more I think about it . . . well, I'd like to practice with you, but . . .'

" 'Will, you're a fool,' the other said. 'The Middle West is a cheap place to study medicine, but no place to practice it—nothing but small towns and farmers— none of them with any money. You'll never make a dime out here.'

" 'You're probably right, Ben.'

" 'Well, then, come east with me. We'll travel in Europe, hobnob with all the greats of the world. We'll meet beautiful, rich young women. With our talents we can't miss,' the other persisted.

"Will was silent for a moment, then said, 'It's a

tempting picture you paint, Ben, but it's just not what I want. I want first of all to be a great surgeon— the very best, if I have the ability—'

" 'And you will be,' the other interrupted. 'What's wrong with getting rich in the process?'

" 'Nothing, I suppose. But what about these people here? They need good doctors too—even if they can't always pay. No, I think I should go back home to Minnesota and give them all the help I can.'

"Some weeks later they parted—Ben going on to New York with his dream of getting rich treating the wealthy and powerful of the city. Will headed for Minnesota where he would be a horse-and-buggy surgeon, helping his father, a general practitioner, the two of them ministering to the sick in the small towns and farms in and around Rochester.

"In the years that followed nothing much was heard of the young doctor with the dream of getting rich in New York. As for young Will, he, with his younger brother, Charles, developed the Mayo Clinic from a small clinic founded by their father in Rochester, Minnesota, in 1889.

"Eventually Will Mayo did treat the wealthy and powerful from the East, just as his college friend had wanted. But he did not go to them in New York. They came to Rochester."

You and I come from a divine source. When we understand and serve that truth and our own potential, great things can happen.

Second, as Oliver Wendell Holmes once stated: "Truth is tough. It will not break, like a bubble, at a touch." Truth can take as much as we can give it. The problem is that sometimes we don't have the courage to really test it. But, then again, some of us do.

A fellow educator tested the toughness of truth (and himself) as a member of the staff of a reputable religious college. He was not of the same faith as those on the faculty, but he was invited to speak at the daily chapel service. His first inclination was to talk on some general Christian principle, but he had recently heard comments on campus about his own religion not being considered Christian. As he thought and prayed about what to do, he determined that the prejudice had to be met head-on. With some uneasiness and fear, he spoke forthrightly in defense of the central message of his religion and his belief in Christ. There were some raised eyebrows and cold shoulders, but the response of the students and most of the faculty was very positive. Many of them began to more carefully examine their own beliefs and values.

Often we are afraid to cast truth into the jaws of opposition, but it is my experience that the truth will not break.

Third, and again from Mark Twain, "When in doubt, tell the truth." The truth is so vital! So use it! I have seen the results of its use so often in my own life and in the lives of my family and friends. One such friend, the president of one of our nation's great universities, shared a tender moment in his personal life with his family:

"One night I came home quite late from work. My nine-year-old daughter, Mary, seemed visibly distressed. . . . I asked if she felt all right; she nodded that she did; but I guessed otherwise. I waited as she got ready for bed. Sure enough, she walked softly into the living room and said, 'Daddy, I have to talk to you.' I held her hand and as we walked into her bedroom she started to cry.

" 'I was at Grand Central this morning and saw a ladies' compact I knew Mother would love. I was sure it was quite expensive but I picked it up just to admire it.' More tears and struggle to get it all said. 'It fell out of my hands onto the floor. I quickly picked it up but, Daddy, the mirror was cracked. I didn't know what to do! I didn't have enough money to pay for it and I was all alone. . . . I put the compact back on the shelf and left the store. Oh, Daddy, I think I've been dishonest.' And then she wept and wept.

"I held her in my arms as that little nine-year-old body shook with the pain of sin being expelled. She said, 'I can't sleep and I can't eat and I can't say my prayers. What will I do? I won't ever get it out of my mind.'

"Well, Mother joined us and we talked quite a while that night. We told her that we were very, very proud of her honesty . . . and we would have been disappointed if she had been able to eat or sleep very well. I told her . . . the compact probably wouldn't cost too much, and that we would go back to the store manager, tell him of the problem, and, between the two of us, cover the cost. If the compact was still there, [perhaps we could] buy it for Mom. That little cracked mirror could be a reminder for as long as she owned it that her little girl was unfailingly honest and spiritually sensitive. . . .

"The tears gradually stopped, her little body began to relax, and Mary said, 'I think now I can say my prayers.' " (Jeffrey R. Holland, *Ensign*.)

What a lesson! Remember Mark Twain: "When in doubt, tell the truth."

Fourth, let's turn to Sir Winston Churchill, who said, "Men occasionally stumble over the truth, but most of them pick themselves up and hurry off as if nothing happened." That's the challenge—running into truth and recognizing it. Now, how does that happen? May I suggest that some of the ways it occurs are when we:

1. Really love our husbands and wives and admit it.

2. See ourselves as we really are and don't reject it.

3. Hear truth spoken and accept it.

4. Recognize beauty and don't deny it.

That's just a sample—the list goes on and on.

As you and I find truth, whether we trip over it or are sincerely searching for it, we can and ought to use it. Marvelous things will follow. The Savior said, "And ye shall know the truth, and the truth shall make you free" (John 8:32).

Nothing brings greater freedom than the truth, for with truth we are free from ignorance, bigotry, and sin. We are free to pursue our happiness now and our eternal life in the world to come. We are free to laugh and be happy.

May I conclude this chapter by once again stating the four pillars of truth: Truth is, in reality, the most valuable of gifts; it is, verily, tough as nails; it is, truly, the best and safest course to follow; and finally, it is, everlastingly, always in front of us if we care to capture it.

It is my hope that we will always seek truth and be wise in our use of it. May we use it to bless our own lives and the lives of our family members. As we do so, may we be patient with those who have not yet discovered its importance.

10

Healthy Is Wealthy and Wise

A young college man went to his spiritual leader and asked for some counsel. "I'm miserable," he said. "Nothing in my life is going right. I am doing poorly in my classes this semester. I'm depressed all the time. I can't do anything well. I can't even seem to pray anymore. My life is totally out of control. What can I do?"

Well, you might expect that his leader would have started to give the young man lots of advice on self-discipline or trying harder or setting goals or something worthwhile like that. But he didn't. He just asked the student three pertinent questions—three questions that were, just then, the missing key to his spiritual development. And you won't believe what they were! He asked: "Are you getting enough sleep? Are you eating well? Are you exercising?" The boy shook his head to each question, and his friend said, "For a month sleep regularly, eat well, and exercise daily, then come back and we'll talk about your problem."

But after that month there was no need for the young man to come back for, miraculously, with good care of his body, his emotional and spiritual frustrations seemed to disappear.

Well, of course, there is no money-back guarantee that your deepest problems can be solved by good health, but it is true that our overall well-being is more closely linked to our bodily condition than we often believe. You may want to face each day with energy and zest, conquer each problem with self-confidence, explore new spiritual frontiers, but it is certainly difficult, if not impossible, if your body drags you down because it is tired and without strength.

Writer Bert Fairbanks noted: "Health isn't just the state of not being ill. Health is the ability to use the body to perform all needful activities; health is strength, vigor, endurance, and a robust appearance; health is lack of fatigue, the ability to think and make decisions quickly, unhampered by physical lethargy; health is bringing the body to the same level of perfection to which the Lord admonishes us to bring our spirits." (Bert L. Fairbanks, *A Principle with Promise* [Salt Lake City: Bookcraft, 1978], pp. 4–5.) "And the spirit and the body are the soul of man," said the Lord (D&C 88:15). The spirit and body! After your resurrection, for all of eternity you will have both spirit and body. That's a good reason for learning now how to care for that body.

Your body can be an obstacle or a blessing to your progress, and it is really all up to you which it will be. Now, there are those who live by the myth that you can do anything to yourself as long as it doesn't hurt somebody else. "It's my body," they say, "so what!" That's been the time-honored excuse for all kinds of bodily abuse. It's the phrase that drops from the drug addict's mouth as he indulges in his habit.

It's on the lips of the high school girl who tried a little alcohol. But who are they kidding? Their bodies aren't fooled by that ready excuse and neither is the world. Our society pays dearly in higher crime rates and deteriorating neighborhoods for its drug-addicted members; alcoholism takes a miserable toll in shattered families, welfare rolls, and automobile accidents.

In the fullest sense of the word, our bodies aren't really ours, anyway. They are sacred vessels created by the Lord and given to us for a time as a stewardship. We are to care for them, preserve them, nurse them, and ultimately be accountable for our custodianship of them. The next time you abuse yourself with fatigue or forgo exercise in the name of saving time, ask yourself how well you are taking care of your assignment from the Lord. How well are you caring for his creation? Your health has a tremendous effect not only on you and your progress but also on your family.

What kind of exercise do you get? Homer Ellsworth said: "A few generations ago, exercise was something that came naturally. The man who worked in the field or the quarry, who rode a horse regularly and walked long distances as a regular part of life; the woman who washed clothes for hours on a scrubbing board, or churned butter, or walked miles doing her marketing—they had little trouble staying physically fit. However, they usually had diets far inferior to what we have now and medical science didn't have the ability to fight disease. It seems ironic that today, with medicine and nutrition enough to live far longer than our ancestors, we also have labor-saving devices that shorten our lives."

Modern life allows us to use up precious gasoline instead of using our muscles that need the work. We ride everywhere we go, insulated by steel and chrome against the world when our bodies yearn to be out in it. How many of us ever do anything that allows us to use our full strength? Our pent-up energy accumulates and spills out in frustration instead.

What is good exercise for you depends on your age, but a general rule of thumb is that an effective exercise is one that raises your pulse rate to about 130 beats per minute for those over fifty years of age, or to 150 beats per minute for those under fifty, and then keeps it there for at least fifteen to twenty minutes. In other words, good exercise is the kind that may leave you puffing a bit. It takes this kind of stimulation of your heart and muscles to send the oxygen out through your lungs into your blood-stream to nourish every individual cell of your body. Cells without oxygen die. Cells with oxygen flourish. Of course, check with your doctor for the exact and safest heart rate you should use.

Don't fool yourself into thinking you are too old to start exercising. This is the perfect time for you, whether you're twenty-two or eighty-two. Physicians have even found that in nursing homes, among those patients who were senile, physical exercise and mental stimulation brought about markedly im-proved health conditions. And, speaking of age, it is startling to see two people of the same age who look twenty years apart in appearance. Often the differ-ence is that one has let his body become beaten and worn out with disuse and another has stayed physi-cally active. What do you want to look like in twenty years? You're deciding every day.

And what do you want to look like next week? You're deciding that every day, too, by what you eat. We have become a nation of dieters as we all try to live up to our bony ideals. But eating well is important, not just to get you into a smaller size, but because it affects every aspect of your physical well-being. Americans have more food and more kinds of food available to them than any people in the history of the world. But with all this bounty, we still manage to be undernourished and fat. We still, willingly, take harmful substances into our bodies that destroy them bit by bit, cell by cell. Every pound of fat you carry, every soft drink you add to your middle, makes your heart work harder and puts a greater strain on this organ whose duration is not endless. To get the maximum vigor from our bodies, we need to learn how to eat well but not overeat. If you are one of the millions of Americans who are always on a diet but never lose any weight, consider some of the reasons why you may tend to indulge.

Do you eat impulsively, running madly for the refrigerator every time you feel nervous or tired? Do you blame others for your own overeating or blame a situation such as Thanksgiving or a birthday party? One overweight man announced to his family that there weren't going to be any more holiday goodies until he lost his weight—no trick-or-treating, no Christmas cookies, no birthday cakes. That was an interesting way to avoid taking blame for his own problem. Do you simply say, "I don't care; my body doesn't matter"? Do you use food as a means of self-indulgence because you deserve it? Do you eat too much as a punishment of yourself, an expression of self-hatred? Do you allow food to become a substitute gratification when you do not receive adequate love or attention? Food! We consume pounds and pounds of it every year, and it is not always because we are hungry.

In the short run, your body may not rebel when you eat improperly, but in the long run you will notice a dramatic difference in your total well-being.

Regular exercise, good food, and sound sleep are three necessities for emotional well-being and spiritual progress. They are not to be ignored.

The Lord has asked us to stay healthy and it is, surprisingly, a spiritual commandment. He said, "Wherefore, verily I say unto you that all things unto me are spiritual, and not at any time have I given unto you a law which was temporal" (D&C 29:34). It is my hope that we all may learn to live the rules of total health so that we can progress as we should.

11

Become a Learner

If the only learning you've accomplished lately is to compare amounts of pain reliever in the leading aspirins as you watch the television set, it's time for a change. Those shelves in your house weren't meant only for knickknacks and plants; they were meant for books! And your mind wasn't meant to hold only advertising jingles and the list of things to do each day; it was meant to treasure up the history and philosophy, the poetry and experience of all mankind.

These days, then, when most of our wings have been clipped with the high price of goods, why not discover the world from your armchair in the pages of a book? It's a fascinating world! Do you know that the Arabs have a thousand words that mean *camel*? In Tibet, some people buy their milk supply frozen on a stick and let it thaw at home before using. And do you know that when the moon is overhead, because of its gravitational pull, you actually weigh less? (That's when I weigh in!)

Speaking of the world, most of us feel great pity when we hear of those in less fortunate areas who are illiterate. But Mark Twain had something to say about that: "The man who does not read good books has no advantage over the man who *can't* read them." None of us may like to think of ourselves as illiterate, but the overall effect is just the same if we do not read. Everyone was born ignorant, but if you stay that way, you have only yourself to blame. Einstein and Edison, Newton and Curie—not one of them was born with any more knowledge than you have.

Our lives will grant us only a snip from the grand cloth of experience. We will know only that which we can observe and feel firsthand, unless we decide we want something more—such as confidence and breadth and understanding. How are we to understand the uncoordinated facts of our world if we have nothing to judge them by? How can we assess current events if we do not understand the great forces that have shaped history? How can we wield an influence in the world if we know nothing about it?

Reading pushes back the boundaries of our experience. Too many of us these days are bored. We may be busy, but we're bored all the same. We may find that when we're alone, we are not in great company. Our minds wander over and over again down well-worn paths. Our thinking is slow and muddy. We are not challenged to explore new frontiers within our souls. Instead we chitchat with ourselves; we look for excitement in a fresh sensation rather than a fresh thought. We live on the surface of things when at our very fingertips, as close as the nearest library, is a repository of man's noblest thoughts.

Andrew Carnegie said, "A man's reading program should be as carefully planned as his daily diet, for that too is food, without which he cannot grow mentally." Walt Disney commented: "There is more treasure in books than in all the pirate's loot on Treasure Island. . . . And best of all, you can enjoy these riches every day of your life." Unfortunately, for too many of us, our school diplomas were just death certificates of the mind, for that day we folded up shop and called ourselves educated.

I hope I haven't just described you—but if I have, there's still a chance. Why not put yourself on a reading program? As one writer said: "A person reading well-selected books becomes a denizen of all nations, a contemporary of all ages. In books one meets all kinds of people—the wisest, the wittiest and the tenderest."

Setting aside just fifteen minutes a day will enable you to read up to two dozen average-length books in a year. Keep it up and you will have read one thousand books in your lifetime. That's the equivalent of going through college five times.

Remember, it was in books that all the ideas that have stirred and fired mankind for good or ill were first penned. "In Turgenev's *Fathers and Sons* he depicted for the first time in fiction the nihilist who was the forerunner of the Communist; dictators in every age have found much (unfortunately) useful advice in *The Prince,* where Machiavelli declares it proper for a statesman to commit in the public interest acts of violence and deceit that would be reprehensible in private life; if non-Germans had taken the trouble to read *Mein Kampf* when it was published in the 1920s, they would have found Hitler's entire programme spelled out in all its shocking detail; it was half a century after Thoreau's death before his doctrine of civil disobedience was applied by Mahatma Gandhi in India." The most celebrated equation in history, $E = mc^2$, was first published by Einstein in an article on atomic energy.

For mankind's glory or defeat, there they are, all the ideas that man finds when he pushes to the very farthest reaches of his genius. Jane Austen's community of gentlefolk, Mark Twain's South of a century ago, Tolstoy's Russia at war—there they are, waiting for you to be moved by them, angered by them, expanded by them; there they are, waiting to make your mind ever more supple in assessing truth and comprehending experience. Can we even fathom the power of an idea?

But, of course, the important question is how we select the books we will read, and this is where most of us fall dismally short. We often choose badly. As the monthly letter of the Royal Bank of Canada noted: "To spend time on naughty narratives in a world that holds Hugo and Dickens and Toynbee, Shelley and Shakespeare and Churchill is like being told you may have your choice of all the diamonds in Tiffany's and then walking out with a bit of broken glass. Or, as Ruskin put it: 'Will you go and gossip with your housemaid or your stableboy, when you may talk with queens and kings?' " This reminds me of something my father told me once about talking: "Paul, small minds talk about people, large minds talk about events, and great minds talk about ideas." And, of course, those ideas very often come from the books we read.

Many of us, however, do not know which are the great books and which are not, and if any two people were to list the most important books ever written their lists would probably differ considerably. For guidelines, however, you might check to see if your library system has a recommended reading list. You might call the nearest university's English or history or humanities department and check to see if they have reading lists of the best books. Some books have

even been published that recommend lifetime reading plans. Your plan may be different than any of
these—your list will probably reflect your reading
tastes, which are always highly personal—but do try
to stretch yourself with your reading. Don't just stick
to books that are easy or comfortable or familiar. It's
only when you have to reach a bit that you are
growing.

One married couple developed an interesting
reading plan. Together they chose a subject to concentrate on for six months and read all the books they
could find on it. During one six-month period they
studied Beethoven, his life and music. In another,
they read about American art. One book led to
another; their conversations were exciting and stim-
ulating. They became sort of "mini-experts" in the
fields they explored. They soaked their minds in the
many points of view expressed about their topics,
and thereby clarified their insights on the matter.

You will probably find in your reading that every
good book leads to another. Read a piece of literature
and soon you may want to know about the history of
the period in which it was written. Read a piece on
modern politics and soon you may find yourself
checking its bibliography for other books that may
amplify your understanding of the problem.

Now, of course, you're probably thinking that all
of this is fine and good for the country gentleman
who has nothing to do, but you—you have no time
for reading. Might I say that touching base with the
great minds of the world may take less time than you
think. Norman Vincent Peale tells us about a man
who read all of Gibbon's *The Decline and Fall of the
Roman Empire* in the intervals of waiting for his wife to
dress for dinner. We all have snatches of time like
that during the day when we can read—on the bus, at

the lunch counter, just before bed. As I mentioned earlier, if you spend just fifteen minutes a day, you can read at least twenty average-length books between January first and December thirty-first.

Finally, with all your good reading, don't forget the finest reading of all—the scriptures. We read them not just because they are masterpieces of writing, but because they are true. Even the keenest minds of this world fall far below the understanding of the Lord.

Take the leap! Be a thinker! Start to read! That we may do so is my hope for us all.

12

The Book

Because she was greatly distressed by the ignorance of the people in the small village in which she was vacationing, an old lady persuaded the schoolteacher to give some reading lessons to some of the less literate adults. One day the lady was walking down the street when she met one of the new pupils. "Well, John, I guess you can read your Bible by this time," she said.

"Bless your heart, ma'am," was the grateful reply, "I was out of the Bible and into the baseball news over a week ago."

Well, how many of us think we've outgrown the Bible and are on to other things? Too many! I asked a friend of mine the other day if he'd been reading the Bible lately, and he said he didn't need to—he'd already seen the movie. It does seem that a scriptural illiteracy is creeping through our society. People read everything—the funnies, the best-sellers, the labels on soup cans—but most simply don't read the scriptures. If we have copies in our libraries and can quote a few key passages, we call ourselves well versed. But, let me ask you frankly: how well do you know Habbukuk? When was the last time you read Paul's epistles? the book of Revelation? Most of us carry the illusion that we know a great deal about the gospel, when in fact we haven't thoroughly studied the Lord's word.

Carol Lynn Pearson wrote a humorous poem she calls "The Lord Speaks to a Literary Debauché Newly Arrived in Heaven." It goes like this:

> Impressive indeed, this shelf of books
> On which all the earth-critics dote.
> But oh, my son, how I wish that you
> Had read the book I wrote.
> (*Beginnings*, 2nd ed. [Salt Lake City:
> Bookcraft, 1985], p. 27.)

In her verse "Moment of Truth," Ora Pate Stewart writes:

> "Children, the minister's coming soon,
> And the parlor looks erratic—
> Lena, I want you to take all the books
> That we never read to the attic."

> Carpets were beaten—the dusters flew—
> And soon everything was in order.
> They killed the red rooster and made a pie
> For the "unexpected" boarder.

> "He's coming! Johnny, go take his horse,
> And remove the saddle and bridle."
> "Shall we have a word of prayer, little flock?
> Will someone bring me the Bible?"

> "Lena, bring him the Bible, dear."
> There followed a moment of static,
> "But Mama, you said to take all the books
> That we didn't read to the attic."

The Lord has told us that to return to him we need to "press forward, feasting upon the word of Christ" (2 Nephi 31:20), but most people choose instead a starvation diet. They barely nibble at the scriptures and call it sufficient. If there were a sealed book that contained the very secrets of existence, the whys and wherefores of our even being here, everyone would fight for access to it—to join the elect few who were permitted to view its pages. But the scriptures, which contain messages of power and understanding almost beyond human comprehension, are taken quite for granted.

During the war in Vietnam, some of the Americans who were taken prisoner reported that they hungered for the words of truth found in scripture more than they hungered for food or freedom. They yearned for the understanding of their higher nature and destiny; they wanted to be assured that the Lord loved and stood with his children through their trials.

Now, there are many reasons to read the scriptures. When Senator William E. Borah, one of the great orators of the United States Senate, was asked why he read the Bible, he replied: "I read the Bible, particularly the New Testament, to learn how to say what I feel must be said clearly, distinctly, and with effectiveness. The Bible writers didn't waste words. . . . The Bible has helped me, more than anything else I've read or studied, to speak effectively using a minimum number of words to convey my ideas, with vigorous, descriptive words."

Another young man, who was later to become president of the United States, was also an avid Bible reader. As a boy, it seems he entered an essay contest in which the challenge was to write a history of the United States during its first century and a half, stressing those factors that had exerted force on the development of the nation during that period of time. This was the catch—the essay could not be more than five hundred words in length. Many entered the contest, but they found the guidelines impossible to meet. Young Calvin Coolidge, however, won the prize handily. His explanation was that his competitors simply hadn't studied the Bible. He threw out a challenge to anyone to tell the story of the good Samaritan in fewer words than are contained in the biblical account of this parable without omitting any part of the recorded story. Coolidge thought knowledge of the scriptures was indispensable to the learned person. Certainly the Bible is the great heritage of our race, a carrier of culture, history, and literature unequaled by any other nonscriptural volume.

But there is a far more important reason to read the scriptures, both ancient and modern. Christ told us what that reason was, saying of the scriptures that "they are they which testify of me" (John 5:39). We've been sent to earth to be doers of the word, but how can we do the word if we have not first heard it? Sometimes mortality frustrates us. We feel blunted, somewhat powerless, cut off from the Lord. We utter prayers, often wondering if they have merely echoed in our heads. We want desperately to understand who the Lord is, what he can do for us, and what he expects of us. We'd like to slice through all these layers of blindness and the daily activities which seem to keep us bound. There is something deep in our very nature which seems to whisper that there is more.

It is only through scripture study and prayer that we can gain a higher concept of the character and will of our Heavenly Father. In the pages of scripture, we see intimately how he grooms his children for their best growth. As we read his words and admonitions again and again, the light of our understanding opens. Principles we thought we understood suddenly take on a new dimension. We suddenly have eyes to see and ears to hear what the Lord is trying to teach us.

"They are they which testify of me," he said of the scriptures. Isn't that really what our hungry souls are yearning for—to begin to have the divine nature revealed to us, to begin to perceive clearly those things which we now perceive only in part?

The Apostles of Jesus Christ required long exposure to him during his earthly ministry before they could even begin to comprehend him. Peter had seen Christ take the lifeless hand of a child and raise her from the dead. He had supped with Christ and walked with him. He had dared to step on the treacherous waves of Galilee to follow him in faith. And it was only after all that, that Christ could pose him the simplest question, "Whom say ye that I am?" (Matthew 16:15.)

Each of us must find that answer for himself, and the finest way to do that is to study the scriptures, giving ourselves long and in-depth exposure to them, accompanied by prayer. Heavenly things reveal themselves at no less cost. It takes the kind of refining that constant scripture exposure gives us to make us ready to receive such things.

As a postscript, I offer some quotations demonstrating the impact of the Bible on the lives of some famous people:

"The Bible is the rock on which the Republic rests."

—Andrew Jackson

"The first and almost the only book deserving of universal attention is the Bible. I speak as a man of the world to men of the world, and I say to you, 'Search the scriptures. . . .' The earlier my children begin to read it the more confident will be my hopes that they will prove useful citizens of their country and respectable members of society."
— John Quincy Adams

"I believe the Bible is the best gift God has ever given to man. All the good from the Savior of the world is communicated to us through this book."
— Abraham Lincoln

"Inside the Bible's pages lie all the answers to all the problems man has ever known. I hope Americans will read and study the Bible. . . . It is my firm belief that the enduring values presented in its pages have a great meaning for each of us and for our nation. The Bible can touch our hearts, order our minds, and refresh our souls."
— Ronald Reagan

"The circulation of the Holy Scriptures has done more, perhaps, than anything else on earth to promote moral and religious welfare among old and young."
— King George V

"The Bible is worth all the other books which have ever been printed."
— Patrick Henry

"If we abide by the principles taught in the Bible, our country will go on prospering and will continue to prosper; but if we and our posterity neglect its instructions and authority, no man can tell how sudden a catastrophe may overwhelm us and bury our glory in profound obscurity.''

—Daniel Webster

13

Grow Up as You Grow Old

Not long ago a young woman approached me and said, "I'm twenty-nine today."

"I didn't know it was your birthday," I answered.

"It's not," she grinned. "Tomorrow's my birthday and this is the last day of my whole life I'll ever be able to say honestly that I'm only twenty-nine. I think I'll decorate the house in black crepe paper for the occasion."

Well, in our culture everybody hates to turn thirty and most hate even worse to turn forty or fifty, or (heaven forbid) sixty-five. As H. A. Overstreet said: "One of the fatalities of our culture has been that it has idealized immaturity. Childhood has seemed to be the happy time."

Now, if childhood is the only happy time, most of us are in big trouble, because not one of us can escape the fact that he is growing older every day. Don't be fooled into thinking it just won't happen to you, because it will. The sad thing about this business of

time passage is not really the growing older, but the
fact that many of us grow older without growing up.
Because we don't seek maturity we don't know what
it means. If, for example, someone should call a
woman mature, she might take it as an insult. In
truth, "The richness or poverty of our lives depends
upon our maturity." And it's time we knew just what
maturity means.

Scientists have been examining the question of
maturity in what they call the Grant Study. They
have picked a group of college men who graduated
from an eastern university in the early 1940s and have
followed their development ever since with periodic
questionnaires and interviews. Dr. George Vaillant,
who has analyzed the study, said: "I first began to
interview the Grant Study men at their 25th reunion.
I was 33; they were 46. . . . Afterward, I was alarmed
by what I had learned about the next decade of life
and I rushed to discuss my experiences with my
54-year-old department chairman. 'I don't want to
grow up,' I explained to my chief. 'These men are all
so . . . so depressed.' " But Dr. Vaillant had more to
learn about these men. Most of them said that the
period of life they were then in, the period from
thirty-five to forty-nine-years old, was the happiest in
their lives to that point and, surprisingly, they re-
garded the period from twenty-one to thirty-five as
the unhappiest. Another thing Vaillant began to discover is that all of them had experienced a consider-
able number of problems in their lives. The healthiest
among them admitted that they were sometimes
frightened, depressed, even disillusioned.

Interesting! Most of us believe we are the only
ones with obstacles to face and hurdles to overcome.
Oh, we may recognize that there are a few others
with dramatic difficulties, but mostly our own
troubles seem so humdrum, nagging, and constant,

like a box within a box within a box. They just never let up. It sometimes seems that life is out to break our hearts.

The immature among us believe that life's problems can be solved and put away like packages on a shelf. Such people wait to really live and grow until the pressure has subsided or the problem has been neatly tied and put away. They seek escape, trying to avoid what seems to be their lot. But problems are never neatly tied and put away, and there is really no escaping. Just as one has subsided, another comes, and we find ourselves always having to respond to the shifting and sometimes stormy weather conditions of our lives. Just as the scenery accompanies the journey, so endless challenges accompany this life. It is true for everyone, no matter how easy his lot appears.

So how do you handle it? That is the glory of maturity. Mature people have stopped blaming this or that for their troubles and have faced them head-on with creativity and courage. As one writer said, "The young may build themselves imaginative castles, but as part of their maturity they learn to take off their coats, go into the quarries of life, chisel out the blocks of stone, and build them with much toil into the castle walls."

Not long ago a curly-haired three-year-old went running headlong into the corner of a kitchen cabinet, splitting open her forehead with a two-inch gash that went straight to the bone. She responded just as you'd think a three-year-old would. She doubled up her fist, hit the wood, and said through her tears, "Stupid cabinet!" Clearly the cabinet, not herself, was at fault for her injury.

As children, the Tudor kings of England were not punished for their misbehavior. Instead other children were employed and used as whipping boys.

Their job was to take whatever corporal punishment the princes deserved for a misdeed.

Some of us today wish we had our whipping boys. But we don't. We cannot blame our problems on our families, on our bad luck, or on society. We cannot delude ourselves into believing they will disappear. Mature people claim responsibility for themselves and their lives. They plant the flag that says, "This is me and mine," and in so doing they are granted a curious power to face and conquer what they must.

Aristophanes, the great Greek playwright, made fun of Socrates in his drama *The Clouds*, and all of Athens seemed to be laughing about it. Socrates went to see the play and when his caricature came on stage, he stood up so that the audience might better enjoy the comic mask that was designed to burlesque him. Now, that's maturity.

Dorothy Carnegie points out another example of maturity: "Alexander Graham Bell once complained to his friend, Joseph Henry, head of the Smithsonian Institution in Washington, D.C., that he felt hampered in his work because of a lack of knowledge of electricity. Henry didn't sympathize with Bell or say, 'Too bad, son. Too bad you never had the chance to study up on electricity.' He didn't attempt to make it easier for him by saying that Bell should have had a scholarship or more help from his parents. His only comment to the young man was, 'Get it!' "

And, of course, Alexander Graham Bell did get it, and that knowledge helped make him one of the benefactors of all mankind in the field of communications.

The Apostle Paul reminded us of the importance of maturity when he said, "When I was a child, I spake as a child, I understood as a child, I thought as a child: but when I became a man, I put away childish things'' (1 Corinthians 13:11).

May each of us find the exuberance, the serenity, the wisdom to grow up as we grow old.

14

Moving Targets

Several years ago while concluding basic training in the military, I had to learn how to fire many different kinds of infantry weapons. The M-1 rifle was quite different from the Browning automatic and the .30 and .50 calibre machine guns. These were all different from the 60 mm mortars or the anti-tank guns. While learning to fire the M-1 and Browning automatic rifles I had to learn the difference between stationary and moving targets. Hitting a moving target is much more difficult than hitting one that is standing still. I soon learned that when I shot at a moving target I had to "lead" (aim) ahead of the mark. After many attempts and much practice, it became somewhat easier.

In my experience of shooting at moving targets I can see some current and practical applications to life. It seems to me that if we are going to discover greater joy and happiness in this world, we will need to learn how to aim a little bit in front of our targets. We will need to look down the road to see what the consequences are for the bullets we are about to fire. If we don't, we may very well aim too high or too low and, in the process, injure some innocent person or even ourselves.

Paul, in writing to the Corinthians, gave a great thought about such consequences when he said: "Take heed lest by any means this liberty of yours become a stumblingblock to them that are weak" (1 Corinthians 8:9).

When we don't look ahead of our actions, we can inadvertently hurt those around us. Unfortunately, those hurt are often the ones we love the most.

Remember with me the unfortunate death of TV and rock star Ricky Nelson. I can remember him as a fun-loving son on the TV show "Ozzie and Harriet." Many of you will remember him as a singer of some renown. I also recall Ricky because of a statement he made as a teenager. He observed: "As far as I have been able to find out, older people have been complaining about the wildness of kids for centuries. My father insists his generation was exposed to the same type of criticism that we are today. I just don't understand why the accused so often have turned into the accusers."

What Ricky didn't understand then was that as we mature we start shooting ahead of the target; we start looking down the road at the consequences of our actions. When we do that, we often get accused of being the accusers. I think another name for that kind of thinkers is "concerned parents."

When we celebrate Christmas, we often see portrayed on television the story of Scrooge in Dickens's marvelous story *A Christmas Carol.* Do you recall the central theme of that tale? Thanks to supernatural intervention, old Scrooge was allowed to see where and what he would be if he continued his present course. In other words, he saw the trajectory and destination of the shots he was then firing and the deadly results of his poor aim. When he returned to reality, he started shooting ahead of the target with vision and understanding of the consequences. What a marvelous lesson to be learned!

I sometimes wish, probably selfishly, that before we fire off a shot, or commit an act, we could immediately be warned of the consequences to ourselves or others. However, it might be embarrassing if that little warning were to occur with many people around us. It would be a little bit like the feeling described by a former great hockey goalie, Jacques Plente, who once teased, "How would you like a job where, if you made a mistake, a big red light goes on and eighteen thousand people boo?"

Having experienced that feeling myself in the sports in which I have participated, I have some appreciation for the life of a goalie. And, thanks to a wise Heavenly Father, our agency is not hampered by the blaring of warning signals and the flashing of lights.

Some years ago I read a story of a man who understood both Paul's counsel and the principle of aiming ahead of the target. The story concerned a poor family living in New York just before World War II. It is the account of a father and mother and their teenage son:

"For weeks a new Buick Roadmaster had stood in the window of the biggest store on Main Street. Now, on the final gala night of the country fair, it was to be raffled off. After watching the fireworks I stayed in the shadows at the edge of the throng for the climax: the drawing of the winning number. Draped in bunting on a special platform, the Buick glittered under a dozen spotlights. The crowd held its breath as the mayor reached into the glass bowl for the lucky ticket.

"Never in my most extravagant yearnings had it occurred to me that Lady Luck would smile upon the only family in town without a car. But the loudspeaker boomed my father's name! By the time I had wormed my way up to the platform, the mayor had presented Dad with the keys, and he had driven off amid cheers and 'The Stars and Stripes Forever.'

"I made the mile home in record time, seeing myself at the wheel of the Buick driving my girl to the senior prom. The house was dark, save for lights in the living room. The Buick stood in the driveway, glistening in the glow from the front window. . . .

"Panting from my run, I touched the car's smooth surface, opened the door and got inside. The luxurious interior had that wonderful new-car smell. I studied the gleaming dashboard. Turning my head to revel in the cushioned vista of the back seat I saw my father's sturdy figure through the rear window. He was pacing the sidewalk. I slammed the door and rushed over to him.

" 'Leave me alone!' he snarled.

"If he had clubbed me over the head, I could not have been more hurt. Shocked, I went into the house.

"Mother met me in the living room. 'Don't be upset,' she said. 'Your father is struggling with an ethical problem. We'll have to wait until he finds the right answer.'

" 'What's unethical about winning a Buick?'

" 'The car may not be ours after all. There's a question.'

"I shouted hysterically, 'How can there be a question? It was announced downtown over the loudspeaker!'

" 'Come here, son.'

"On the table under the lamp were two raffle stubs, numbers 348 and 349. The winning number was 348. 'Do you see the difference between the two?' Mother asked.

"I looked carefully. 'The only difference I can see is that 348 won.'

" 'Hold 348 to the light and look hard.'

"It required a lot of looking to see the faint letter *K* dimly marked in pencil on one corner. 'Do you see the *K*?'

" 'Just barely.'

" 'It stands for Kendrick.'

" 'Jim Kendrick? Dad's boss?'

" 'Yes.'

"She explained. My father had asked Jim if he wanted to buy a ticket. Jim had mumbled 'Why not?' and turned back to what he was doing. It may never have crossed his mind again. Dad then bought two tickets in his own name with his own money, marking 348 for Kendrick, a scarcely discernible thin mark on one stub that could be obliterated by the lightest rub of a thumb.

"To me, it was an open-and-shut case. Jim Kendrick was a multimillionaire. He owned a dozen cars. He lived on an estate with a staff of servants, including two chauffeurs. Another car meant less to him than a snaffle on Barkis's harness meant to us. Passionately I argued, 'Dad's got to keep it!'

" 'I know he'll do what's right,' Mother said calmly.

"At last we heard Dad's step on the front porch. I held my breath. He went straight to the phone in the dining room and dialed. Kendrick's phone rang for a long time. A servant finally answered. From what Dad said at our end I could tell that Kendrick had to be awakened.

"He was annoyed at being roused from sleep, and far from pleasant. My father had to explain the whole thing from the beginning. The next afternoon Kendrick's two chauffeurs arrived in a station wagon. Before driving the Buick away, they presented Dad with a box of cigars.

"We didn't get a car until after I was grown. But, as time went on, my mother's aphorism, "If you have character, you have the better part of wealth,' took on a new meaning. Looking back over the years, I know now we were never richer than we were at the moment when Dad made that telephone call." (John Griggs, "The Night We Won the Buick," *Reader's Digest*, May 1979, pp. 162–63; originally published in *Remember, Remember*, ed. Lynn Thibodeau, copyright 1978 by Carillon Books.)

Thank heaven for great fathers and mothers who can aim before they fire, who know how to "lead" a target, and who are unafraid to look down the road at the consequences.

May I also be so bold as to suggest that adults are not the only ones who aim ahead of the target. I know of many young children who do the same. And there are plenty of teenagers who defy the mold we adults would often put them in, who aim well ahead of their targets.

I have a good friend whose seventeen-year-old son recently did just that. This young man had worn his hair longer than his parents wanted him to. As the mother's birthday grew close, this young man asked her what she wanted for a present. You guessed it—a haircut. Why? "To set a good example for your brothers and sisters." Now, although we may not agree about whether short hair really proves anything at all, to this special mom, it did. She was asking him to aim ahead of the target. Well, he did!

He cut his hair short. That alone was a great gesture of love, but this particular boy also took some physical and verbal abuse at school. His blacked left eye proved it. But as soon as his friends saw that he would not be intimidated, they left him alone. (The fact that he flattened one of them didn't hurt any.) Can you imagine the effect of all this on his mom and dad? his younger brothers and sisters? his friends? His aim was perfect—ahead of the target. The consequences of his agency will be profoundly felt for years to come. I salute him.

We can all learn to shoot ahead of our targets—in fact, we must. Our willingness to look down the road will make all the difference. My target practice during basic training helped save my life several times. Our continual practice of shooting ahead of the targets we face may very well save our own eternal souls and the lives of those around us.

I close with a verse by Robert Frost:

> I shall be telling this with a sigh
> Somewhere ages and ages hence:
> Two roads diverged in a wood, and I—
> I took the one less travelled by,
> And that has made all the difference.
> (From ''The Road Not Taken.'')

When all around us are firing indiscriminately, may we take careful aim on the future.

15

Style

Not too long ago a personal friend of mine passed away—a great man, a renowned scientist, a person for whom I have great admiration. He had been highly honored during his lifetime for his scientific achievements, both in the United States and abroad. But above all else, Henry Eyring was a teacher and a friend of youth. He was a genius in the classroom and, in addition, was very close to his students in such everyday activities as sports and campus frolics. For a man his age he was in excellent physical condition—even in his sixties, Dr. Eyring could do a standing broad jump from the floor to the top of his desk. He got great pleasure from challenging and participating with his university students in thirty- or forty-yard foot races, some of which made the local television news . . . and rightly so.

One day just a few years before Dr. Eyring died, one of his close friends, upon meeting him in a local city building, noticed that he was carrying a cane. The friend quizzed, "Henry, what is the cane for?"

And Henry Eyring replied, "Style, President, style." What a classic response!

I submit that this great man did, indeed, have style. He lived that way and he died that way.

Recalling this wonderful quality and presence about him, and especially remembering the account of the cane, I again checked the dictionary for the definition of the word *style*, and I found that it certainly fits Henry Eyring and those like him. According to Mr. Webster, style is simply "overall excellence, skill, or grace in performance."

As a young baseball player, I once had the honor and challenge of pitching against Joe DiMaggio, the great center fielder for the New York Yankees. He had what I call style. He was a superb athlete who played baseball with deceptive ease. He was one of the all-time greats.

He made the hardest catch look routine, and when he was at bat, he hit with tremendous power but never appeared to be exerting himself. He made everything look effortless, although what he did could only be achieved with great effort. Once when asked why he played so hard, he said, "I always thought there was at least one person in the stands who had never seen me play, and I didn't want to let him down." Now, that is style—"overall excellence in performance."

"The battle of Antietam was fought Sept. 17, 1862, during the American Civil War. In no other battle of that war were so many killed and wounded in a single day. The fighting began early in the morning and was so intense that troops of General George B. McClellan's army had no opportunity to fall back to the rear for food. As the day wore on, the soldiers became faint with hunger.

"The commissary sergeant of one of the regiments, a young man of nineteen, felt so strongly his responsibility to feed his men, regardless of the danger to his own life, that he decided to take the food to the front lines himself.

"He took two mule teams, loaded wagons with food and drinks, and started for the firing line. Over the treacherous ground he drove in spite of numerous warnings to turn back. When his mules were shot from the wagons, he picked up others and continued his perilous journey to the front. There he fed every man in the regiment a warm meal, 'a thing,' said his commanding officer, 'that had never occurred under similar circumstances in any army in the world.'

"The strict sense of responsibility which this young sergeant had developed prepared him to perform many other significant services for his fellow men in the years that followed. In 1882, he was elected president of the United States. His name was William McKinley." (*Instructor*, January 1958.)

There it is again—"overall excellence in performance"—in other words, style!

It's all around us: Family members with style, friends with style, leaders with style, followers with style, the young with style, the old with style. Age makes no difference. Gender makes no difference. Status makes no difference. It's available to all.

Joseph Haydn, that matchless musician, was present at the Vienna Music Hall, where his oratorio "The Creation" was being performed. Weakened by age, the great composer was confined to a wheelchair. As the majestic work moved along, the audience was caught up with the tremendous emotion. When the passage "And there was light!" was reached, the chorus and orchestra burst forth in such power that the crowd could no longer restrain their enthusiasm. The grandeur of the music and presence of the composer himself brought that vast assembly to its feet in spontaneous applause. Haydn struggled to get out of his wheelchair. Finally up, he motioned for silence. The enraptured crowd heard him call out with what strength he could muster, hand pointed toward heaven, "Oh no, not from me, but from thence comes all!" Having given the glory and praise to the Creator, he fell back into his chair exhausted.

There it is again—style! Excellence in whatever we are called upon to do is as possible as we believe it can be—no more, no less.

Near the battle's end at Waterloo, as Napoleon could see he was losing, he summoned a Highland bagpiper. He said to the young lad, "Play a tune." The boy did. "Now play a march." Again the boy responded. "Now," the general commanded, "play retreat."

"I can't," said the boy, "I don't know how." What an outstanding response!

During a World War I battle it was Field Marshal Ferdinand Foch of the French army who also showed style. Surrounded by the German army and with no possible route of escape, Foch was ordered by headquarters to take the offensive. The field marshal's reply: "My center is giving way, my right has been penetrated, my left is wavering, the situation is excellent. I *shall* attack!" What class! What style!

As I have considered the subject of style and have pondered the experiences of Henry Eyring, Joe DiMaggio, William McKinley, Joseph Haydn, Napoleon, and Field Marshal Foch, I have wondered what it is that sets these great individuals apart from their contemporaries. How can we become as they are? Do we have to be sports heroes or great composers or scientists to qualify? The answer is obvious but hard to put into words. I found it one night as I sat and did what I call "fun reading." Zane Grey said it: "To bear up under loss, to fight the bitterness of defeat and the weakness of grief, to be victor over anger, to smile when tears are close, to resist evil men and base instincts, to hate hate and to love love, to go on when it would seem good to die, to seek ever after the glory and the dream, to look up with unquenchable faith in something evermore about to be, that is what any man can do, and so be great."

That says what I consider real "style" to be all about. It really does describe "excellence of performance." Look again at Zane Grey's statement:

1. To bear up under loss (even when it's a loved one).

2. To fight the bitterness of defeat and the weakness of grief (especially when it happens at home).

3. To be victor over anger (especially with our loved ones).

4. To smile when tears are close (and even after they come).

5. To resist evil and base instincts (even teenagers can pull it off).

6. To hate hate and love love (especially when it concerns family members).

7. To go on when it would seem good to die (some of us can understand that one).

8. To seek after the glory and the dream (especially as we get older).

9. To look up with unquenchable faith (it can be done).

Well, that's style. It takes practice and effort and pain, but it's worth the price—and more. And Zane Grey was right, "That is what any man can do."

Remember, there is one thing about genuine style —it never goes out of style. May it be so with us.

III

Warming Trends:
Extending
Love to Others

16

The Only Gift

I sat in a restaurant one day and watched a young family as they came in—a father, mother, and three small children. They were seated at a table near mine and I could easily overhear some of their conversation. The small children were what I have come to expect kids to be—somewhat restless, wiggly, and very normal. But for some reason the dad was overly impatient. Finally, in exasperation, he shouted at his children, "Shut your mouths and hold still! If I hear one more word out of any of you I'll knock your heads together!"

Now, to be truthful, I have edited the father's language. He used words that I recognized from my career in the military—vulgar, biting language. In addition, he gave them a look that would have melted steel, the kind of look no child should ever receive. The mom was horrified; those all around them were embarrassed. The whole experience was a travesty. I was seriously tempted to write a message and hand it to the mother as I walked out. It would have read something like this, "Madam, we were all equally embarrassed with you, but thank God the children have you!" Well, I didn't write it.

As I have considered that experience, and as I have counseled with many hurt and abused people, both old and young, my heart resonates to the words of the Savior, "A new commandment I give unto you, that ye love one another; as I have loved you, that ye also love one another" (John 13:34). Ralph Waldo Emerson put it in different words: "Rings and other jewels are not gifts, but apologies for gifts. The only gift is a portion of thyself." That makes a lot of sense to me.

We all have a common father—a Heavenly Father. We are all his children. Whether we are aware of it or not, we are all brothers and sisters. We are related. We are family! (Maybe that's why we treat each other the way we do sometimes.) But everyone has a right to be treated as a child of God, a brother or sister. Everyone deserves kindness. Everyone, you say? Yes, everyone! I admit it isn't easy to treat everyone with love and kindness, but that's the way it ought to be. And that's the way it can be!

Kathryn Fong tells an interesting story about how she learned that giving a "portion of oneself" can be rewarding:

"I had never truly experienced the joy of giving. . . .

"So far in my young life, it seemed, I had failed to give of myself beyond the call of duty, even though I prided myself in giving some degree of compassionate service: baby-sitting, chauffeuring, helping in a crisis situation. But these were mediocre extensions of myself which deserved only modest praise and approval.

"Not that I was looking for a ripe occasion to be benevolent. Not by a long shot! Age twenty-two was a reasonably sound, selfish age. But time and fate were conspiring to give me an opportunity to change my attitude. . . .

"Each day I rode the regular commuter coach from Hayward to San Francisco, and joined the throngs of office workers hurrying to their daily routine of earning a living. . . . My hide was toughened to endure the pushing, jostling sea of people. I was a true San Francisco commuter; I enjoyed the unheralded distinction of being alone in a crowd. Certainly no one would *dare* require anything of me during this period of the day.

"Until I met *him*. 'He' was not a real human being to me—but a decrepit, whiskey-guzzling wretch, a beggar with a stench that merited neither attention nor pity. He was dressed in the season's latest panhandler ensemble: black trousers torn at each knee, with frayed cuffs; grey-green T-shirt complete with air-conditioning vent holes; a woolen shirt of undetermined color, whose buttons obviously had come from someone else's shirt; and a thin, dirty jacket. A pair of wooden crutches supported his frail body. A worn baseball cap managed to keep some of the rain off his bewhiskered face.

"My automatic pilot commanded me to jam my hands into my pockets, offering no small change for his extended hand. . . . I held firm to the code of honor among the bands of commuters. I did not give in.

"I quickly forgot this small interruption in my day, only to have it repeated several mornings later. Then, one chilly morning as I passed the freezing beggar, my conscience began to stir and the Ghost of Christmas Past began to speak from the distance. I shifted uncomfortably and reasoned that I was not responsible for his human annihilation—it was his error in life, not mine. Besides, what could I possibly do for him? I had no power to make him well and whole again. Yet the man's image pricked my cold armor sufficiently to form a chink right where my heart was. I had to admit I was sorry for the poor wreck.

"And with this remarkable show of feeling, I expected my conscience to accept and withdraw. It didn't. When I walked into church on Sunday, I was smothered in feelings of hypocrisy and guilt for my lack of concern. Every conceivable emotion and gospel virtue bullied me with salvos of Christian demands. Finally I responded to the promptings of my heart. I would help this poor creature.

"But how? I could not help to salvage his life by shoving money into his grimy palm. He would only ravage himself with more liquor. Well, then, how about food? That was it. I would pack him a hearty lunch. When was the last time he'd enjoyed a brown bag lunch? The only thing he would carry around in a brown paper bag was a bottle. I wondered if he remembered what a ham and cheese on rye was like.

"Carefully I coordinated my image of a big hungry man with a three-pound, solid, three-course meal, which I shoved into the refrigerator with satisfaction that night. In my prayers, I told my Father in heaven my strategy, as if he and I were plotting a surprise party.

"Monday morning, as I approached the corner the old man had inhabited for nearly two weeks and prepared to extend my offering, my heart was pounding with the goodly rhythm of human kindness. And I was greeted by a blank wall. He had gone—walked out on me—deserted! This skid-row personality who had haunted me for nearly two weeks had dared to vanish.

"In disappointment I quickened my step and began what I knew would be a rotten day. It was. And the next and the next. Two weeks went by, and I had decided to forget about my act of charity. Then one day as I walked impassively toward the street corner, my eyes darted beyond the *Don't Walk* sign—and there he was! Nothing had changed. He was his old filthy self, staggering to support himself on his crutches, his hand extended for the day's alms.

"My first impulse was to ignore him. Besides, I had no hefty lunch to offer. 'But you have an orange in your purse,' my conscience spoke.

" 'Yes, I do,' I retorted, 'but what would he do with an orange?'

" 'Give it to him and see,' my conscience battled.

" 'No. No, I don't want to.' But my conscience took over and guided my hand to my purse to rummage for the orange. It was a great physical contest; I hesitated as I approached him, but in the end extended my hand and put the orange into his palm.

"I paused and looked under the bill of the baseball hat. His eyes remained fixed on the orange for a second, and then slowly he raised his eyes to mine— the prettiest blue eyes I had ever seen, set in the filthiest face. They were Paul Newman–blue eyes, amid a network of livid red and white. His mouth began to move, but no sound came. I smiled. He nodded and clutched the prized orange to his chest. No words were exchanged. None were necessary.

"There on the corner of Mission and Fremont streets in the city of San Francisco, the spirit of giving, the Ghost of Christmas Past, and the angels who herald Christian acts applauded long and loud in my heart. The beggarman gave me a great and treasured gift. I knew what it meant to give.

"I took a long, deep breath and turned away, still smiling. My steps resounded on the pavement as I continued my trek. Suddenly my eyes were open to the street scene, my ears heard the accompanying sounds, and I smelled the conglomerate odors of an early San Francisco morning." (Kathryn P. Fong, "The Orange and the Tramp," *Ensign*, December 1977, pp. 34–35.)

Isn't that a marvelous story? If I knew the name and address of my distant friend in the restaurant, I would send him a copy.

Giving a portion of ourselves is indeed a gift. But we need to remind ourselves that gifts are not all necessarily received in the spirit in which they are given. All that you and I can do is give. It's up to whoever receives the gift to accept it or reject it. And when we give of ourselves and we're rejected, it's not easy to take—at any age. Such was the experience of a young lad whose account is told by an unidentified writer:

"The game of cowboys and Indians had been going on vigorously, and to stretch the meaning a little, peacefully, out on the beach for some time. Then suddenly, there was trouble.

"One of the youngsters, a brown-haired cowboy, about seven and the youngest of the lot, had been captured by the Indians and was to be tied to a stake —the stake being a huge, ugly hunk of driftwood that looked very much like the gnarled roots of an ancient tree. The brown-haired cowboy objected to being tied to the driftwood. Whether, in his concept of the game, the driftwood was not legitimately a stake or whether he, out of some special sensitivity, found the ugly driftwood objectionable, I could not make out. But he was very definite about it, he would not be tied to it.

"The boss of the game, the oldest of the boys, about ten or eleven and something of a bully, grew angry.

" 'Go on home, yellow!' he shouted at the little fellow. 'Go on home. We don't like you!'

"The other boys, in the natural spirit of the gang, took up the words in sort of singsong. 'Go on home, yellow! We don't like you.'

"The boy, hurt and bewildered by this sudden show of cruelty, looked from one face to another. Then, after a long moment, in a voice quavering but deeply earnest, he said, 'But I like you.'

"The singsong stopped before his earnestness. For a brief moment, it seemed as if his simple but gravely moving words would have some effect. Three of the boys looked at one another in uncertainty. They had been somehow touched.

"The bully had not been touched. 'Go on home, yellow!' he cried out again. And then to the gang, 'Come on, fellers! Let's go!'

"The game was begun again without the brown-haired cowboy. He looked desolately on for a minute or two, then turned and moved slowly away, following the frothing white line of the sea's edge, sadness in his drooping figure, bewilderment still on his sensitive face.

"I watched him go. I felt profoundly sorry for him. It was as if I had just watched the stoning of a prophet.

"He grew smaller in the distance. Still his words stayed with me. 'But I like you.'

"He disappeared from my view around a wide sweep of the shore."

It's a long way from Galilee to the beach in Malibu, but there are some striking similarities. It was Lavater who said, "The manner of giving shows the character of the giver, more than the gift itself."

As I conclude, may I suggest that, ordinarily, when we give a portion of ourselves, the gift is accepted. On occasion the giver himself might even be rewarded, and with more than just the good feeling that giving brings. I chuckle as I remember one such incident:

"I was driving to a job interview and running 15 minutes late when I saw a middle-aged woman stranded with a flat tire. My conscience made me stop. I changed her tire and headed for the interview, thinking I could just forget about getting the job now.

"But I filled out the job application, nevertheless, and went to the personnel director's office. Did I get the job? Sure thing! The personnel director hired me on the spot. She was the woman whose tire I had just changed."

Yes, giving does occasionally have some immediate rewards.

Let's consciously decide to give a little of ourselves every day. It can be in small, seemingly insignificant gestures. It can be to our moms and dads, husbands and wives, brothers or sisters, friends or strangers. But if each of us decided to do some small act of kindness every day, think what effect it would have on families and communities everywhere.

May you and I give the only gift that really counts: ourselves, for if there is anything better than to be loved, it is to love.

17

A Tonic for Tired Parents

You know, children would be brought up perfectly if families would just swap kids. Everyone knows what to do with the neighbors' little ones! But you may not feel that way about bringing up your own children. In fact, you may spend a whole lot of time not knowing what to do at all. Child rearing is one of those things that seems so easy looking on and so boggling in the thick of it. A simple thing like trying to get your children to pick up after themselves can become a civil war. Making the bed can become an all-morning project. And tell me what a parent is supposed to do when a toddler comes in across a just-vacuumed floor with two cuffs full of sand!

But the real reason I think it would be so much easier to raise our neighbors' children is that we don't care about them so much. We simply wouldn't feel that overwhelming sense of responsibility. Parents have been told so often that their children's very character is in their hands for molding that parenting may seem as gloomy as being assistant store manager in charge of raising prices. The job may be necessary, but it's not much fun.

Every parent wants to rear children who are responsible, brilliant, obedient, and polite. And every parent half wishes he could just pull the right string and have his child respond in kind. But it doesn't always happen that way and everybody knows that. Sometimes the harder you try to help your children grow and do good things, the harder they resist you, and the tension between you can sometimes erupt into bitter words. "You look awful," a mother says to her toddler who insists on wearing stripes with plaids, or to the teenage girl who wears jeans for everything but sleeping. "Don't you ever learn?" a father may ask when his son presents him with his third traffic ticket that year. Parents don't mean to, but sometimes they say horrible things to their offspring—things like: "That was a dumb thing to do," or "How many times have I told you?" These things we sometimes say only because we love our children so much; we care so much; we hope for so much in their lives.

A young mother was talking to one of her friends on the phone, and as they talked, they exchanged pleasantries, told interesting stories, and laughed heartily at the joy they felt in each other's company. Finally, the conversation ended and the mother's small boy got his turn to talk. "Why don't you ever laugh with me?" he asked.

The mother thought about it for a minute. She helped the boy with his piano lessons, took him to soccer, laundered his clothes; every mouthful of food he ate she had purchased and prepared with hours of her time—and all he had to say was, "Why don't you ever laugh with me?"

Children sometimes say profound things, and this little boy had. Sometimes parents try so hard to rear good children that they forget to enjoy the process. For some of us it all becomes such serious business, complete with orders, directives, and scowls. When do we step out of the pattern and just laugh? How often do we just talk, throw a ball, play a game? There should not always be that bitter edge between parent and child that says to the child that he's being watched. It's that edge that keeps him self-conscious, miserable, and uncommunicative around his parents.

You who are parents, step out of that pattern for a minute and really look at your child. There is so much to enjoy in him. The Lord made only one like him. He didn't come from a cosmic Xerox machine. There are no other copies, and even tomorrow he won't be like he is today. The shine may be gone from his eyes and replaced by older worries. The giggles will be swallowed up in maturity, the bounce controlled, the gaps in his mouth from missing teeth filled. A small child never returns. Once he's gone, you won't find him again if you search the whole world over.

So, I'm going to say something most shocking about child rearing. Once in a while—be a little careless, be a little carefree. Stop the car when you are hustling somewhere with your child and look for rocks or chase butterflies. Take his childish interests to heart. Let him wreck the kitchen for an afternoon searching for some secret in chemistry. Just once—get on the bed and jump with him. Run through the sprinklers when you've a hundred better things to do. Make him laugh. Laugh yourself! Isn't it funny that just having fun may be the most important thing you ever do?

Let me share the experience of a young woman who taught in an inner-city school of a big eastern city. This is what she said: ''It doesn't sound hard to face a class of sixth graders, but these children were unlike the soft, giggly children I'd known in my neighborhood. At sixth grade, they were already street-wise and street-weary, and I soon learned it was impossible to control them with any conventional discipline. They laughed or catcalled when I talked; they threw spitwads at each other. Nothing I tried seemed to work. I'd threaten to expel them for their bad conduct; I told them I'd flunk them for their test questions left empty. One day I even called the vice-principal into class and let him chew them out. Nothing helped. It became evident to me that in any contest of wills I was bound to lose. No punishment I could mete out was as bad as what many of them had already faced. They were tougher than I was and I knew it. And what was worse—they knew it.

''At last,'' said this young teacher, ''I had to learn this basic law of living. You cannot *make* anyone do anything. By force of your own will, by discipline or threat, you cannot make a strong-willed child obey you or grow into something bigger than himself. He has to *want* to. And there's only one way to make him want to. Love him. Enjoy him. Make it much more rewarding for him to please you than to do anything else. Children can unfold into miracles when they think somebody wants them to, but everybody resists being controlled.''

Now, what does that have to do with having fun with your child, laughing with him? Everything! You may find that your child will blossom into that responsible, obedient, polite person you had in mind more readily because you loved him than because you constantly corrected him. Love is the most powerful, irresistible force in the universe in changing lives. Listen to his long explanation about the beetles he found on the way home from school. Listen to his music, and because you did, he may be willing to listen to yours.

But most of all, have fun! The best writers are those for whom writing is more fun than eating ice cream. The best company presidents are those who think it's a ball to direct people and programs. And the best parents are those who think it's really great fun—not great work—to be with their kids. In fact, we are all kids, grown just a little taller.

18

A Child's-Eye View

One day a little child was holding an ice cream cone that started to drip down the sides and all over his fingers. His father didn't notice the drips until the boy's hand was covered with sticky melted ice cream. "Look what you've done," the father shouted in exasperation. "Why don't you use your head?" The son gave his father a strange look and then wiped the ice cream from his fingers all over his head. He did just what his father said; he'd used his head!

Another child had her own little disaster. Her mother told her specifically not to play past the corner, yet time and time again the mother came out and found the child way down the street, far past the corner. "I told you not to go past the corner," said the mother, all ready to spank the child. Just before she got the first blow in, the child looked up, whimpering, and said, "What's a corner?"

Did you ever get the feeling, as these two parents did, that you were not communicating with your children? Most of us do sometimes. It's not uncommon to hear a parent shouting, "If I've told you once, I've told you a hundred times not to do that!" And I'm sure all hundred times the command was repeated the child and the parent were miserable. So often it is hard for us to understand why our children can't simply do what they are told. Why can't they just measure up to our best expectations of them? Is that so hard to do, after all?

Well, children have been frustrating adults for centuries. A cartoon in an 1872 copy of the magazine *Punch* shows a mother saying to an older child, "Go directly—see what she's doing and tell her she mustn't." It was the noted Charles Lamb who said, "Boys are capital fellows in their own way . . . but they are unwholesome companions for grown people." Much of the frustration that adults may feel toward children comes because the adults get so locked up in their own pressures and concerns that they can't understand what the world looks like from a child's point of view. A child seems to be that person who is dirty when he ought to be clean; he is the one who spills when the table is set with the best linen; he messes up the house when it ought to be orderly; he wants things his own way when his parents want them their way. He is a bother for all seasons. Right? Maybe not!

One year a household arts show in Paris had a surprising exhibit in its home furnishings section. It was a room filled with giant-sized furniture to show what children have to put up with in a grown-up world. A photographer followed a model around to record her problems. He discovered some interesting things. Do you know why so many children have dirty hands? Even if they are tall enough to see over the sink, they cannot reach the faucet. Why do children spill things at the table? The model found out that one child-sized hand won't even fit around the neck of a milk bottle. Why do they never hang up their clothes? Who can reach those hangers way above their heads? And why don't they sit still? Well, how can you be still when your feet don't reach the floor?

Obviously, the problems between parents and children are not all so clear, but the room of giant-sized furniture at the household arts show does point out that our children live in a different world than we do. Even teenagers with their adult-sized bodies see the world from a wholly different perspective. If we want to talk to them, to be their trusted confidants, we have to climb out of ourselves and try to understand what it's like to be them. How do they feel? What makes them hurt? How do they view us?

One expert on child psychology, Dr. Haim Ginott, said that our normal talk drives children crazy—the blaming and shaming, preaching and moralizing, ridiculing and belittling, threatening and bribing, evaluating and labeling. We have to eliminate such critical comments as: "When will you learn?" "What's the matter with you?" "How many times have I told you?" "Didn't you hear me?" We need to replace those comments with some honest listening.

One mother was grieved because she just couldn't seem to get through to her son. Finally, someone suggested that she spend a couple of days just listening to the kinds of things she said to him. At the end of her listening time, she reported, "I had no idea I never spoke to Jimmy except to admonish him or order him to do something." That's how most of us talk to our children: "Do this. Do that. Don't do this." We rarely sit down and just let them talk to us. They need us to listen so much. Some of the most important things that will ever happen to them, some of the impressions that will color their thinking when they are eighty years old, are happening right now, right before our eyes.

One adult man once confessed to his wife that the most painful thing that had ever happened to him was not making the ninth grade all-star basketball team. Does that sound silly? Oh, it's not that he hadn't had plenty of disappointments and losses since then, but that particular disappointment had come when he was especially vulnerable. What had probably appeared too unimportant to the adults in his life at that time was a terrible, heart-rending blow to him.

May every parent who has ever loved a child take this message to heart. Remember that there is someone smaller or younger who needs you to listen to him. There is someone who needs you to set apart a special time for him. No business appointment or urgency, no chore or distraction is nearly as important as your child. Who is this miracle unfolding before you every day? Discover now, before your child is grown and gone.

Society today is pressuring your child in ways unknown even ten years ago. On television he'll see casual immorality and ready violence. He'll see hundreds of examples of people flying in the face of authority and downgrading traditional values. Your child will feel pressure on every hand to rebel against your teachings, to embrace the wonderful promise of unfettered freedom. If you are to protect him from this storm of contradictions and lawlessness with which our world is being bombarded, become his trusted friend, the first one he turns to with his big secret to tell, the one he comes to for sharing his little joys. Then you must become someone he wants to emulate.

When I hear parents say of rebellious teenagers, "I just don't know what's become of that child!" I think that their rebellion didn't happen all at once. It didn't happen just yesterday. Somewhere along the line true, caring communication broke down between the parent and child. Too many times when the child came to talk, the parent just didn't have the time. He dismissed the child as a casual annoyance. He thought the little needs were trivial, the little accomplishments unimportant. This may not always be true, and not every parent with a child who disappoints him should blame himself, but all of us must beware of equating the size of the child with his importance. Our children look to us in special ways because they are helpless. If their dependency upon us sometimes seems overwhelming, it is because their need for us is so great.

A beautiful young lady said that when she was thirteen she had a problem and went, unexpectedly, to her father's office. He was the president of a large corporation. Upon being told that he was too busy to see her, she rushed home, flung herself on the bed, and cried. Mother, hearing her sobs, came into the room. "Daddy doesn't love me!" she blurted out through the tears.

The next day while at school the young lady received a call from her father's private secretary. "Could you come to the office at four o'clock today for a visit with the president?" said the secretary. The girl was thrilled and the appointment was set. At four o'clock she was ushered into her father's office with as much pomp and ceremony as the richest client.

There, her father told her to sit in a brand-new chair located next to his desk. Then he said, "That is your chair. Whenever you have things bothering you, come and sit in that chair and I will drop whatever I am doing and listen to you and help you because I care about you more than I care about anything in this world except your mother and brothers and sisters." "And," the girl reported, standing radiantly before a group of her peers, "he never once broke his promise."

Mothers, fathers, may you make the time to be that kind of parent—to sit and listen, to climb out of yourself and see what it is like to be five again, or ten, or sixteen. May you have the inspired imagination and composure to do so.

19

Improving Basic Training

While visiting the home of a family member recently, I was greeted by one of the youngsters who was seeking refuge from an attacking brother. As she sought safety between my legs, I couldn't help but think of a similar situation.

"Jack's mother ran into the bedroom when she heard him scream and found his two-year-old sister pulling his hair. She gently released the little girl's grip and said comfortingly to Jack, 'There, there, she didn't mean it. She doesn't know that it hurts.'

"She was barely out of the room when the little girl screamed. Rushing back in, she said, 'What happened?'

" 'She knows now,' Jack explained. (*On the Up Beat*, vol. A, No. 8B, 1986.)

Oh yes, home can be the greatest place on earth, but there are times when "heaven on earth" can occasionally be a little hectic. I suppose homes in reality are meant to be training camps and not always resort hotels. I recall with much fondness when, as a young father, our home seemed to take on the characteristics of a basic training camp. When you are the only male in a camp of all females, some combat training becomes very useful. I remember well the days of attempting to establish my small beachhead in a bathroom with four women all armed with blowers, hair spray, and other secret weapons. However, like most families, we made it through in admirable shape. As Shakespeare said, "All's well that ends well."

As I often sit with my wife and ponder the delightful challenges of raising three daughters, I have wondered if perhaps we could have done a better job. Perhaps there were many things we could have done to have made the "basic training" less painful. Perhaps having *not* done some things would have helped, as well. I have often remarked that we, as parents, want to help our children in the worst way—and that is what we often do. I have thanked God many times for a wonderful partner who has had the sensibility, understanding, and faith to provide those ingredients I never could. What would we do without the moms of this world? Clara Park penned it perfectly:

> I've heard a lot of good things said
>   about what the pilgrim fathers did . . .
> I wonder who fed them and brought
>   them a drink,
> Kept the children away when they
>   wanted to think.
> It must have been strange with so
>   many others,
> Not to have had any pilgrim mothers.

As far as I can tell, moms are the greatest invention of all time.

With that tribute to my wife, as well as to the millions just like her, I also want to salute the fathers who play similar roles. And my heart continually goes out to single parents, both male and female, who with great love and genius play the role of both parents. Although the ideal is a two-parent family, many human circumstances make such an arrangement difficult, if not impossible. Single parents can and often do fulfill both roles effectively. They should know of our great admiration and respect.

Wouldn't it seem that, regardless of who's in charge, we could make our homes happier with a little more effort? As I think about that question, I believe there is an answer. As in so many instances, the solution can be found in the scriptures. Paul, in his letter to the Colossians, counseled fathers, "Provoke not your children to anger, lest they be discouraged" (Colossians 3:21).

And to the children he said, "Children, obey your parents in all things: for this is well pleasing unto the Lord" (Colossians 3:20).

I think such advice is not only wise but sound. As with most counsel, it is a difficult challenge to know how to put such teachings into practice. It is one thing to say and yet another to do. Keep in mind, Paul tells us not to provoke our children to anger. That does not mean we shouldn't discipline. Discipline—firm, but loving—is basic to the well-being of a child. Children seek direction and want proper restraints.

I recall the story of a seven-year-old boy who was given the assignment of feeding the family cows each night. Like most boys, he did well for a while but soon reverted to his seven-year-old ways and the cows went hungry. Now, some parents would be tempted to discard Paul's advice and take their children to the woodshed. But this boy had wise parents who understood the principle and how to apply it. So, one night at supper they applied the necessary restraint. In the words of the seven-year-old, now a mature adult:

"With the family gathered around the table and the blessing offered, the food was passed—but not to me. The potato dish went counterclockwise around the table to my father at my left, who then reversed its route. The meat took a clockwise route to my brother at my right, but no further. Finally, I realized that there was a conspiracy and blurted out, 'Don't I get to eat?'

"Fully aware of my ravenous appetite, my mother knowingly asked, 'Why, son? Are you hungry?' She graced me with her Mona Lisa smile and added, 'Didn't you have a chore to do when you got home?'

"Then I remembered my important job. 'I'll feed the cows after supper,' I hopefully offered.

"Mom looked straight into my eyes and asked, 'Son, do you suppose the cows are as hungry as you are?'

"Now, that was some question. I hadn't really thought about it. A cow was a cow. At my tender age it had never occurred to me that a cow could be hungry, especially as hungry as I was at that moment.

"Mother continued, 'You go feed the cows, and I'll put your supper in the oven to keep it warm. But you always remember, cows get as hungry as you do. When they are fed, you can eat.'

"I never again forgot to feed the cows." (LeRoy Barney, "Teaching—at Home and Church: Cows and a Pitchfork," *Ensign*, April 1979, p. 14.)

What a wonderful method! Restraint with understanding and firmness is extremely effective. It beats the alternative—screaming, "Get the cows fed, you lazy little twerp!" And that wouldn't help much, anyway! As Paul indicated, that kind of behavior only provokes anger and resentment. Just as certainly, it brings discouragement. Restraint is a wonderful virtue.

I was talking to a teenager the other day about his father and the restraint he uses. This good father not only uses self-control, but also has the good sense and discipline to use the positive approach. This young man told me, "My father is always telling me he loves me (about two or three times a day) and it's hard to be angry when I know he loves me so much."

In my own experience I have discovered that to anticipate a potential problem situation and to seek a solution before it occurs also has a good, positive effect. For example, we often used in our family discussions what I like to call the "we" concept. For instance, we would be having dinner and the topic of discussion might involve a favorite subject of our girls, such as "boys." Before long we would be talking about what boys like and don't like and what a young lady's role was in establishing a proper relationship.

When two of our three daughters were in their dating prime I might have asked, "What do you think is a fair and reasonable time to come home after a date?" Usually a good discussion would follow with some input from Mom and Dad, flavored with much humor. A time would be established—say, twelve-thirty or one o'clock.

Then, while there was no personal or emotional involvement, I might ask: "What should *we*, your parents, do if the plans that *we*, as a family, have decided on are not honored?'' Quite often the penalty they suggested was far more harsh than what we might have devised, such as, ''Ground us for a month!'' It was at that point that *we* could all agree upon an equitable penalty. Then I might have added, ''Should the rule be broken, then you agree that I will put into effect the punishment?'' ''Right, Dad!''

In our family, we usually didn't have to wait too long before someone tested the rule. When that occurred, I could quietly and calmly slip into the bedroom of the offender and say, ''Do you recall the rule *we* made regarding the time you should be home?''

''Yes, sir.''

''Consider the penalty to now be in effect.''

Obviously, exceptions were made in unusual circumstances.

Remember this basic principle of human nature— those who are to be affected by a rule ought to have a part in making the rule. (This assumes, of course, that a child is old enough to express feelings and has some ability to reason.)

Now, what about the children? What was it that Paul said they should do? ''Children, obey your parents in all things.'' Impossible, you say? Not so! I know of many teenagers who not only do it but show others how it can be done. I was discussing the difficulty of this challenge with a beautiful young lady. Her reply was a classic: ''Elder Dunn, I have found that it is not so much how my parents treat me, it's how I treat my parents. And when I try to do my part their response and treatment is wonderful.'' Not bad for a sixteen-year-old!

I can appreciate that some parents are unreasonable in their requests. They ask things that are neither appropriate nor sensible. The Lord has never expected us to obey an unrighteous request. Having authority to preside or rule does not place adults in the role of dictator! Good leaders counsel, suggest, motivate, and inspire. They do not use force or pressure. I believe most parents only seem unreasonable. They ask for obedience in the same way parents have always done. And what does it take to obey? I submit that it's the same for children as for parents: It takes restraint. Instead of yelling something that they will wish they hadn't, young people can learn to hold back and bridle their feelings. They can learn to say, "Sure, Dad, right away," or, "Okay, Mom, I'll get right at it." Such an approach may seem strange at first, but oh, how wonderful the results!

When such methods are employed, family relationships can and do improve. Restraint is the key, restraint exercised by both parents and children. Remember, no change occurs all at once. It takes time and much practice. But as relationships are strengthened, both sides begin to develop the faith, trust, and confidence that we all seek. The following story illustrates such a trust:

"A party of English botanists . . . spent their vacation in the Swiss Alps collecting specimens of rare flowers. They started out one morning from a small village and, after a several hours' climb, came to a precipice overlooking a green valley dotted with a peculiar flower, which, examined through field glasses, proved to be of unusual value. From the cliff on which the party was standing to the valley there was a sheer drop of several hundred feet. To descend would be impossible, and to reach the valley from another approach would mean a waste of several hours.

"During the latter part of their climb a small boy had attached himself to the party and had watched with interest the maneuvers of the botanists. After discussing the situation for several minutes, one of the party turned to the boy and said, 'Young fellow, if you will let us tie a rope around your waist and lower you over this cliff so that you can dig up one of those plants for us, and let us pull you back up, without harming the plant, we will give you five pounds.' [This was equal to twenty-five dollars at that time.]

''The boy looked dazed for an instant, then ran off apparently frightened at the prospect of being lowered over the cliff by a rope, but within a short time he returned, bringing with him an old man, bent and gray, with hands gnarled and calloused by hard labor. Upon reaching the party of botanists the boy turned to the man who made the offer and said:

'' 'Sir, this is my dad. I'll go down in the valley if you'll let my dad hold the rope!' '' (As told at a Primary Convention, June 9, 1934.)

May we be wise enough to seriously consider the marvelous opportunity we have in our homes to train up our children in a spirit of love and understanding, so that when they are old they and their children will not depart therefrom.

20

"Wuv Me"

I have a friend who has a little handicapped boy. This young boy was brain-damaged as a baby and presents a unique opportunity to his parents. The good father loves his son, as he does the rest of his children, but once in a while he finds this son a challenge, especially when he's tired. On one such occasion, after the father had returned home late from work, this special little fellow became determined to get some attention. My friend was equally determined to have some peace and quiet. The son tried every trick in the book—things all children, normal or handicapped, seem to do by instinct. After being rebuffed for almost half an hour, this small boy played his last card. He walked up to his father, threw his arms around his legs, and in desperation and close to tears, yelled, "Wuv me, Dad!" And his father did.

I wonder how many times that same cry has gone unheeded. Don't we all call out on occasion—sometimes in words, sometimes in profound silence? The

disconcerting thing about our modern world is that
the Savior's warning about love is being fulfilled all
around us. He said that where there is great wicked-
ness, "the love of many shall wax cold" (Matthew
24:12).

I suggest, however, that all is not lost. In fact,
there are signs of hope all around. One such sign I
recently encountered is the story of a young minister
who learned about love the hard way. If I remember
correctly, that's the way most of us learn, especially
about love. Walter Wangerin, a newly ordained
clergyman, says one of his real teachers was an old,
black gentleman who lived in absolute poverty and
filth. I think the minister's own words will illustrate
the lesson:

"From the beginning, I did not like to visit Arthur
Forte.

"Nor did he make my job (my ministry! you cry.
My service! My discipleship! No—just my job) any
easier. He did not wish a quick psalm, a professional
prayer, devotions. Rather, he wanted sharply to
dispute a young clergyman's faith. Seventy years a
churchgoer, the old man narrowed his eye at me and
argued the goodness of God. . . . When I left him, I
was empty in my soul and close to tears, and testy,
my own faith in God seeming most stale, flat, un-
profitable at the moment. I didn't like to visit Arthur.

"Then came the days when he asked for prayer,
Scripture, and Holy Communion, all three. The man,
by late summer, was failing. He did not remove himself from the chair to let me in (I entered an unlocked
door). . . . The August heat was unbearable. I had
argued that Arthur go to the hospital. He had a better
idea. He took off all his clothes.

Naked, Arthur greeted me. Naked, finally, the old
man asked my prayers. Naked, he opened his mouth
to receive Communion. Naked. He'd raised the level

of my sacrifice to anguish. I was mortified. And still he was not finished.

"For in those latter days, the naked Arthur Forte asked me, his pastor, to come forward and put his slippers on him, his undershorts, and his pants. And I did. His feet had begun to swell, so it caused both him and me unutterable pain in those private moments when I took his hard heel in my hands and worked a splitbacked slipper round it; when he stood groaning aloud, taking the clothing one leg at a time; when I bent groaning so deeply in my soul. I dressed him. He leaned on me and I touched his nakedness to dress him, and we hurt, and his was sacrifice beyond my telling it. But in those moments I came to know a certain wordless affection for Arthur Forte.

"(*Now* read me your words, 'ministry,' and 'service,' and 'discipleship,' for *then* I began to understand them: *then*, at the touching of Arthur's feet, when that and nothing else was what Arthur yearned for, one human being to touch him, physically to touch his old flesh, and not to judge. In the most dramatic terms available, the old man had said, 'Love me.')" (Walter Wangerin, "The Making of a Minister," *Christianity Today*, September 17, 1982, p. 17.)

There are those words again: "Love me!" Powerful, urgent words! Well, Arthur died shortly after that incident. But like my friend and his handicapped son, the cry was heard—and heeded. Both these men, although in completely different circumstances, seemed to sense the truthfulness of the Lord's admonition, "A friend loveth at all times" (Proverbs 17:17).

Now, as you know, it isn't always easy to love even those we're supposed to love. There are myriads of jokes about those we should love, but we somehow fall short: clergymen, politicians, teachers, mothers-in-law, and the list goes on. One of my friends once indicated that his mother-in-law had just flown into town. Then, with a twinkle in his eye, he added, ''But I told her next time I wanted her to take a plane.'' It's not always easy!

I believe the Lord was serious when he gave us his ''new commandment.'' Let me repeat it: ''Love one another. By this shall all men know that ye are my disciples, if ye have love one to another.'' (John 13:34–35.)

The great thing about the Master is that he has given us both the commandment to love and the means by which to bring it about. We couldn't ask for more. Let me conclude with a couple of the Lord's ''How-to's.'' In speaking of learning to love those around us, Mormon said: ''Wherefore, my beloved brethren, pray unto the Father with all the energy of heart, that ye may be filled with this love, which he hath bestowed upon all who are true followers of his Son, Jesus Christ'' (Moroni 7:48).

Now, that seems pretty plain to me. We ought to get down on our knees and pray that a kind Heavenly Father will give us the gift to love. Even if we're not really sure we want to, we ought to do it. I bear testimony that when we pray for that capacity to love, and we do it with all the energy of our hearts, great things happen.

Second, we ought to get up from our knees and practice: first with our wife or husband; second with our children or parents; third with our friends; and finally with all those around us. But let's begin at home. In reality, charity does begin at home. It's the little things that begin to make a difference: a kind word, a smile, a gentle touch, an unexpected flower given, the dishes done without complaint, the bed made, clothes picked up, a "thank you," a note in the lunch box. Let's express love to all those around us, both in word and deed. Why not tell someone you love him? You may be surprised at the results. Be sure to have smelling salts available. The actual use of those words, *I love you,* can be the salvation of someone close to you.

As my friend responded to those words, "Wuv me!" let us do likewise. I know that such action can bring unspeakable joy to both the giver and the receiver. The Lord expects us to do so, not for his sake alone but also for ours. I know that he loves us as no one else can. And it is my witness that he shows and tells us in myriad ways every day. My prayer is that we may do the same for those who cry out to us.

21

Monuments

If you've ever been to Paris, France, you have probably stood, as I have, and looked in awe at some of the great art treasures of the world. I can remember climbing the narrow stairs to get to the top of the cathedral of Notre Dame. What a beautiful view of the city! I stood with my wife and some friends in the Louvre and admired the picture of the Mona Lisa and the remarkable statue of Venus de Milo. We went to the Eiffel Tower and gazed in wonder as we pondered the engineering genius it took to erect such a thing. We moved from place to place in Paris and saw more than I suppose I'll ever be able to remember. What a magnificent city!

Then we came to the Arch of Triumph and heard the story of Napoleon. The Arch was erected to celebrate the victories of Napoleon and his armies. It was begun before Waterloo and finished after his death.

As I heard the history, I wondered what monument or headstone my family might erect for me when I am gone. I have often smiled at certain epitaphs that I have observed around the world. I recall one that read: "Here lies John Koncupot. May God be as good to him as he would be if he were God and God were John Koncupot." Another stated:

> Mule in barnyard, lazy and sick,
> Jim with a pin on the end of a stick,
> Jim jabs mule. Mule gives lurch—
> Services held at the Methodist church.

On a tombstone in Scotland I read a classic statement telling of the departure of the town's glass blower:

> Liked by many,
> Disliked by few.
> Pity he inhaled
> When he shoulda blew.

Since it is most unlikely that a monument would be considered in my case, perhaps my gravestone inscription might read, "Here lies Paul, he's Dunn." However, I do have some monuments—my wife, my three daughters, their husbands, my grandchildren, my mother, my brothers, my many associates and friends.

I believe that every time we influence those around us for good, we are building a monument to ourselves. No one will have to do it for us. And when Napoleon's Arch of Triumph no longer exists, our acts of kindness, encouragement, love, and caring for our families and friends will still stand, and that influence will be felt in their posterities forever.

Let me illustrate:

"It was a cold January morning, and I was thirteen years old. We lived a mile across town from the school. Since there was no bus, I had to walk to school each day. I had thrown a few snowballs, run a stick along a fence several times to shake off the snow, slid on a patch of ice and, finding it the best so far, spent some time there.

"When I was about halfway to school, I realized that if I didn't hurry, in fact, run most of the way, I would be late for school. As I hurried along, I noticed a rather small figure standing off to the side of the walk, holding onto the fence. As I got closer, I could see that it was a small, elderly lady, and she appeared quite frightened. I was about to rush past her when someone seemed to say to me, 'She needs help.'

"I stopped, walked back, took her gently by the arm, and asked if there was anything I could do. She shakily turned, took my hands, and said she had tried to go for a walk but had nearly fallen on the ice and was afraid to go home alone. As I walked her back to her home, nearly a block away, I thought, 'Well, I will be late for sure now because she is very old and frightened, and she takes small steps.'

"Then I thought, 'She is someone's mother,' and I felt warm inside. I forgot about being late for school. After I had taken her home and helped her safely up the steps to her door, she once again clasped my hands and said in a soft, sweet voice, ''God bless you, my son. I pray that some young man will be there to help your mother when she needs it.''

"A few years ago my father had a serious operation and spent several weeks in the hospital. This was during the winter months. My sons and I had made several trips down to my parents' home to keep the snow cleared from the driveway and walk, but one day while I was working and my sons were in school, we had a very heavy snowfall. My mother was trying to clear the walks when a young university student came by, laid his books down, gently took the shovel from her, and cleared all the walks and driveway. As my mother thanked him he said, 'That's all right. I am away from home going to school. Maybe someone else's son will be there to help my mother.'

"As my mother told me how this young man had helped her, I remembered the words from my childhood, 'God bless you, my son. I pray that some young man will be there to help your mother.'

"And he was." (Max Bonnett, *New Era.*)

There were at least two monuments erected in that story. Lives were influenced for good and forever. No matter what may have happened or may happen after that, those acts of kindness will live forever in the lives of those directly affected and in the influence they will have on those around them.

I remember the words of a great prophet and friend of mine, Harold B. Lee. When called to the First Presidency of the Church, Elder Lee expressed his belief that no one really "replaces" another person in a position. Said he: "We who are called to occupy these positions merely fill the vacancies created by the passing of time. Those who have gone on before still hold their places in the eternal worlds and in the hearts of the hundreds of thousands whom they have served." (Conference Report, April 1970.)

May I repeat those last words, "Those who have gone on before still hold their places . . . in the hearts of the hundreds of thousands whom they have served." Those men and women whose lives have been touched serve as monuments to the greatness of those who did the touching. It will always be so.

May I confide to you a concern I have about this whole subject? The great fear I have is that you and I may not really understand or appreciate the monuments we are building. I see so much good being accomplished by many who are unaware of the eternal implications of that good. I suggest that when we come to understand all that has been done, we'll take heart in the fact that others, not immediately responding or comprehending, will someday know. Some monuments take longer to build.

A fellow teacher, David Parkinson, shares this experience he had with his young daughter:

"One beautiful summer afternoon, in the midst of all of the bustle of preparation for an evening outing with the family, the air was sliced with a high-pitched scream. I recognized it immediately as the distress call of our oldest daughter, Debbie. I hurried to the patio area of the backyard and found her tangled in a heap with her brother's bike. Her scream assaulted my ears as I rescued her. She protectively clutched her left knee, which was covered with . . . blood. I carried her into the house and we quickly cleaned the knee, discovering a cut about eight inches long, beginning above the knee and crossing down over the kneecap. Her mother's statement, 'We'll have to take her to the emergency room!' evoked a new decibel level scream. Debbie did not have a high pain threshold. I became the 'elected' transporter after a temporary taping of the wound.

"The intensity of the screaming seemed heightened within the confinement of the car and I offered a prayer in my heart for assistance for our daughter. I felt certain the emergency room would be ready for us when we arrived, as they would have heard us coming for at least a mile away.

"A thought then entered my mind: Promise her that if she'll ask Heavenly Father to help her that the upcoming procedures at the emergency room would not hurt her. I spent some minutes quieting her enough to present the promise to her. Finally, stifling sobs, she bowed her little head and quietly asked for

Heavenly Father's help so it wouldn't hurt. This seemed to calm her and the screaming did not resume.

"Upon arrival at the hospital, we were asked to wait in a little room with toys and a TV until they could take care of her. Debbie's eyes widened as she jerked her head in the direction of a child's screams coming from behind a drawn white curtain. Her eyes remained fixed upon the curtain as I awaited the seemingly inevitable duet, which, to my amazement, was never formed.

"Soon, a nurse ushered us into the work area and Debbie was seated on a bed next to the . . . curtain (where the screams were heard). From our new vantage point we could see a boy about five years old flaying his arms and legs against the doctor and two nurses as they attempted to subdue him enough to place stitches in his eyebrow and eyelid. In frustration the doctor finally determined that taping the wound was the only alternative to avoid injury to the struggling boy's eye. Debbie watched these events with a frozen countenance but no sounds were uttered. This scene was interrupted by a voice saying, 'Well, what have we here?' Debbie's eyes quickly fixed upon the male nurse who was tugging at the makeshift bandages on her knee. I thought, 'Well, here we go again,' but not a sound. The undivided attention given the nurse would be coveted by every teacher in the Church.

"His next statement, 'We'll have to clean this good,' and his subsequent immersing of cotton into a solution and scrubbing of the wound was destined to return the piercing screams which still echoed in my head; but no sound from her. The nurse said, 'You're a big girl!' I wondered if someone had switched girls; this couldn't be the same one I left home with.

"The nurse left for a moment and returned as I was complimenting Debbie on her remarkable behavior. Which behavior was about to be altered drastically, as I watched the nurse produce a long hypodermic needle, announcing his intent to deaden the area of the wound. Debbie captively watched the administration of that shot directly into the wound and yet made no sound. The nurse's reaction was one of amazement. 'My, what a big girl!'

"Shortly thereafter, the doctor stitched and bandaged the wound, handed her compliments and a sucker, and we were on our way home. As we sat in the car, I asked her why she hadn't cried and her simple answer, 'It didn't hurt!' brought greater faith to the heart of her father and feelings of gratitude to just be a part of the experience."

Now, ordinarily, when we hear a story like that, we extol the faith of the small daughter, and rightly so. But this time I'd also like to compliment a good father. Not only do we see the efforts of a daughter's faith but we see just as clearly the monument built by her father. Who taught this daughter to know and understand such faith? Who cared for her? loved her? taught her to trust in his word? gave her assurance about a kind Father in Heaven?

I believe with all my heart that my colleague's daughter is one of his greatest monuments. And if I am not mistaken, his grandchildren will have similar feelings, as will his great-grandchildren. They will continue to be eternal monuments built to him and his good wife.

Jean Paul Richter tells us, "The words that a father speaks to his children in the privacy of home are not heard by the world, but as in whispering galleries, they are clearly heard at the end, and by posterity." Oliver Goldsmith said, "People seldom improve when they have no model but themselves to copy after.''

Let's continue to teach our children, pray with them, care for them, and continue our family picnics, our softball games, and our trips to the park and zoo. Let's continue to mow the neighbor's lawn, bring his newspaper in from the rain, and avoid kicking his dog. Let's continue putting our arms around the boy with no friends, the girl with parental problems, and the struggling Little Leaguer.

As surely as I live, I know that such a cause will build monuments of eternal value. And, in the process, we will find ourselves someday standing in the presence of a wise Heavenly Father who will recognize and accept those monuments. I sincerely believe the greatest monument we will have built to him will be ourselves.

22

Accents

In my travels, I have talked with people of many countries. Because I don't speak their languages, I've had to communicate in one of two ways: by working through an interpreter or by depending on the amount of English they know. Sometimes when these wonderful people have chosen to test their English on me, it has been a challenge. But of all the challenges I have faced with other cultures, I suppose none has been more difficult than trying to understand the English spoken in a "non-USA" English-speaking country. I remember talking to a group of teenagers in Scotland. They were animated and anxious to share their feelings with me. Generally, I did pretty well and understood the gist of what they wanted me to know. There was one fine young man, however, who spoke so rapidly and with such a heavy accent (or was it me with the heavy accent?) that I could hardly understand a word. I asked him to repeat his statement. He did, and I still didn't get it.

Not wanting to embarrass him (or me) I simply nodded my head and said, "Yes, I see." He seemed satisfied with my response.

Since that time, however, I have worried about what he actually said and what I seemed to give my blessing to. I have occasionally wondered if he told me he was fed up at home and was thinking seriously of leaving town. My approval would not have been in his best interest—or in the interest of his parents.

Accents are critical. By changing the accent from the first to the second syllable, you change the word *perfume* from a noun to a verb. It still costs the same, but the meaning is changed. An accent simply changes the emphasis we place on a word, but what a difference in meaning it can make!

I suggest that life is just like that. Accents are critical. Where we place our emphasis changes the meaning of our whole existence. We can, and do, emphasize the things we consider critical. However, the cost certainly does not remain the same.

"Three hundred and twenty-six school children of a district near Indianapolis were asked to write anonymously just what each thought of his father.

"The teacher hoped that the reading of the essays might attract the fathers to attend at least one meeting of the Parent-Teachers Association.

"It did.

"They came in $400 cars and [$40,000] cars. Bank president, laborer, professional man, clerk, . . . baker, tailor, manufacturer, and contractor, every man with a definite estimate of himself in terms of money, skill, and righteousness or looks. . . .

"The [P.T.A.] president picked at random from [a] stack of papers. 'I like my daddy,' she read from each. The reasons were many: he built my doll house, he took me coasting, taught me to shoot, helps me with my schoolwork, takes me to the park, gave me a pig to fatten and sell. Scores of essays could be reduced to: 'I like my daddy. He plays with me.'

"Not one child mentioned his family house, car, neighborhood, food, or clothing.

"The fathers went into the meeting from many walks of life; they came out in two classes: companions to their children or strangers to their children." (Bryant S. Hinckley, . . . *Not by Bread Alone* [Salt Lake City: Bookcraft, 1955], p. 84.) That's what I call accent.

Let's take a moment and ask ourselves where we place our accent. Where do we place our emphasis? Is it on things? or events? or on people and our relationships with them? What do we really care about?

Well, from the three choices I just gave (things, events, people), I suppose you know what I believe. I think it is also clear to the Lord. It seems to me that our emphasis in life should be on people. For example:

"Tom was a journalist. His newspaper had given him the assignment of traveling to several cities to report some important civic projects, and he had decided to take his wife and seventeen-year-old son with him. He wanted to develop a more meaningful relationship with them, especially his son.

"One hot day they decided to eat their lunch in a public park. As they were eating, Tom said to his son, 'Pass the salt.' His son made no move to comply. Raising his voice slightly he again said, 'Pass the salt.' Again his son ignored his request. Now thoroughly irritated, he raised his voice still more. 'What's the matter with you? I said, *"Pass the salt."* '

"The son got up and left the table. Tom followed him, and as he caught up with him he saw there were tears in the boy's eyes. 'I don't understand it,' said his father. 'What's wrong?'

"It was some time before his son answered. Finally he said, 'Dad, ever since I can remember, we've had a kind of inferior-superior relationship. I don't think you mean to have it that way, but the impression you give is that you think of yourself as being superior to me. Please don't misunderstand me. I know you have more knowledge than I; your experience is much greater than mine, and you have more wisdom. But, Dad, I'm a person, too.

" 'I notice that when we have company for dinner, you never say, "Pass the salt." You always say, "Please pass the salt." That "please" means a lot to me, Dad; it's a symbol of respect.'

"This incident was a great learning experience for the journalist, and it eventually changed his whole relationship with his son. Five years later when the son married, he said to his father, 'Dad, you've changed your attitudes and actions toward me. You've shown real respect during the last five years, and I only hope I can treat any son I might have in the same way you have treated me.' " (*Melchizedek Priesthood Study Guide,* 1966.) It's never too late to change your accent!

People are what is important in life. When we care more about people than anything else, I believe we're well on our way to happiness. However, I would be one of the first to admit that even when we try, if we're not careful, we'll be tempted to leave out some who need our attention the most.

Athletics are a great example of the temptation. I have seen Pee-wee League coaches rant and rave at those little tykes. I've seen them play Johnny because he was a natural athlete, while Jimmy sits on the bench because he's not sure if he's left field or left out. There's a real temptation there. A Michigan high school basketball coach told how this happened to him. His team had won the state championship, and he was on top of the world. Named Coach of the Year, he felt like a hero—until an incident at the end of the school year brought him back to reality. His study hall students were filling out a class schedule for the fall when a shy girl who had sat in the back row all year timidly raised her hand. "Excuse me, sir," she began, "there's one thing I don't know on this form. What's your name?" Stunned, the coach realized that despite all this success, he had failed to reach that girl. She had been in his study hall for eight months, yet he had never taken the time to even talk to her.

Well, there are accents and then there are accents. Where is your emphasis going to be?

I suppose one reason I feel so strongly about accents and emphasis is because of my love for the underdog. I can remember being in that position on more than one occasion in my life. Sometimes it has been when I was on the baseball diamond or being chased by a bully, at times during war, or at other times in a hospital. But I have been there and I know how it feels. So I root for the underdog and try to talk to the shy youngster. I believe that such an accent, such an emphasis, pays dividends.

"In the latter part of the seventeenth century, [a] German preacher, August H. Francke, founded an orphanage to care for the homeless children of Halle. One day when Francke desperately needed funds to carry on his work, a destitute Christian widow came to his door begging for a ducat—a gold coin. Because of his financial situation, he politely but regretfully told her he couldn't help her. Disheartened, the woman began to weep. Moved by her tears, Francke asked her to wait while he went to his room to pray. After seeking God's guidance, he felt that the Holy Spirit wanted him to change his mind. So, trusting the Lord to meet his own needs, he gave her the money.''

Now, if the story ended there, it would be great. We're seeing here not one, but two underdogs. But the story doesn't end there. It never does.

''Two mornings later, he received a letter of thanks from the widow. She explained that because of his generosity she had asked the Lord to shower the orphanage with gifts. The same day Francke received twelve ducats from a wealthy lady and two more from a friend in Sweden. He thought he had been amply rewarded for helping the widow, but he was soon informed that the orphanage was to receive 500 gold pieces from the estate of Prince Lodewyk von Wurtenburg. When he heard this, Francke wept in gratitude.'' (''Our Daily Bread.'')

Whether August H. Francke was German or not, he had an accent. Thank goodness!

I'm willing to admit that few things move me emotionally or spiritually as much as watching someone with an accent, someone who has an emphasis for people, especially the underdog.

Before I conclude, however, I must make it as clear as I can that you can't tell an underdog by his position on the team roster. Some underdogs have money; some have position; some come from wonderful homes. Once again, it's not the things he has or doesn't have—it's what he needs!

Now, since we all have needs, we're all underdogs. We all need each other. We need people who care about people. We need people who have that accent.

It has been my experience that those who have influenced me the most in my life are ones who spoke with an accent. That's the way it will always be.

May we place our emphasis on people. May we reach out, and up, and down. May we reach wherever we need to in order to help each other. May our accent, our emphasis, be on each other. And, finally, may we understand that the Lord himself also speaks with an accent: "Do unto others."

23

Salve

Most of us have had the bittersweet experience of scraping an arm or a leg and then applying the healing remedy—the salve. Have you noticed that sometimes the hardest part of the whole experience is getting the courage to apply the salve to the wound? Children will squirm to avoid it and adults will simply tell themselves the scrape will heal without it. We're great at trying to avoid the salve, even when we know it will help.

Well, there's a type of salve I'd like to mention that's better than the kind we put on cuts and scrapes —and, by the way, it sometimes takes just as much courage to apply. It consists of three words; that's all, just three words. I suppose you're way ahead of me by now. After all, everyone knows the three most important words in any language. As I understand it, those three all-important words are, *I gotta raise.* And next to those come three more of equal import, *I love you.* And then comes the salve—those three words that somehow can heal like nothing else does. Spoken directly, they are, "I am sorry." "*I am sorry!*" Can you just imagine what would happen around this mixed-up world if people started using those three words as a part of their regular vocabulary? Imagine saying, "I am sorry," and meaning it. Imagine hearing, "I am sorry," and knowing it is sincere. Now, that's what I call salve!

I know of a woman who was staying at a big hotel in one of our country's larger cities. When she packed to return home, one of the hotel's washcloths ended up among her things by accident. Unpacking at home, she was horrified to discover the washcloth in her suitcase. "I'll write the hotel tomorrow and return it," she thought, folding it and placing it carefully on the shelf by her other washcloths. Well, like all of us, the next day was a busy one for her and the next week was busy, too, and she didn't think about the washcloth again until she saw her little girl using it to wipe off a chocolate-covered face.

"Oh, no, the washcloth! I'll wash it with my next batch and send it right back to the hotel," she thought.

So with the next batch of laundry she washed the pesky washcloth, folded it and put it back on the shelf, deciding to send the washcloth that very week.

Well, again the week was busy and that month was, too, and the washcloth was used over and over again by innocent family members who didn't know it was stolen goods.

Finally, so much time had elapsed since she had stayed in the hotel she was too embarrassed to write and apologize. She was too humiliated to say, "I'm sorry, but I accidentally took one of your washcloths, and I kept it too." She, who had always been noted for her honesty, began to feel like a thief over a dollar washcloth. She could hardly stand to fold her towels for seeing the washcloth glaring at her among her things. Finally, she could take it no longer. With great relief and some embarrassment she wrote the hotel, sending them a check and a very used washcloth, saying, "I am sorry. I made a mistake." It was the hardest letter she ever wrote, but what a relief she felt to be better once again, unstained by the little guilt. "I am sorry." That's what salve does for us. It heals. And whether our mistakes are accidental or are the result of some weakness in our character, we have to be brave enough and smart enough to own up to them and say, "I'm sorry."

Remember the prodigal son? Here was a young man who thought he knew all the answers and set out to prove it. He demanded his share of his father's wealth and then proceeded to lose it all. Then the famine came and he was left without money or job. Going from bad to worse this young man ended up feeding the swine and almost starving until, as the scriptures say, he came to himself. Realizing his mistake, he rushed back to his father. Now, note his words, "And the son said unto him, Father, I have sinned against heaven, and in thy sight, and am no more worthy to be called thy son" (Luke 15:21).

What that amounts to today is simply, "I'm sorry, Dad. I blew it!" Can there be anything harder to admit—that we are fallible; we make mistakes; we weren't right when we were so sure we were. For the prodigal son, not much else needed to be said. And, happily, this father was wise enough to accept his son's repentance and his apology.

One day while sitting on an airplane headed for a distant place, I was listening to a clean-cut, good-looking young man seated next to me. He was on his way to fulfill a two-year mission for his church. He proceeded to tell me a story much like the story of the prodigal son. He had literally walked out on his parents and ended up in the slums of one of our large western cities. He, too, "came to himself." Realizing what he'd done, not only to himself but also to his parents, he thumbed his way back home and there, on the doorstep of his own home, he knelt and wept. The only words that would come out were, "Oh, Dad and Mom, I'm sorry!" That's all it took.

I have counseled with couples, both old and young, who have finally been able to blurt out the words, "I'm sorry, Honey," and the healing process has begun. I have seen animosity turned to consideration, all because those three healing words were used—"I am sorry." Sincerely spoken, those words can make the difference.

Now, just a word of advice for those who will commit themselves to do better in using the salve. Not all people will be able to accept those words when they are given. Sometimes a parent will not be mature enough to accept an apology and let it go. Sometimes a teenager couldn't care less if a parent tries to say, "I'm sorry!" Sometimes people, being human, won't be able to accept those words at all. But don't let that stop you from trying, because the salve heals both ways—not only the one who receives it, but also the one who administers it. Imagine how different the Savior's life would have been if he had given only to those who had appreciated it!

Now, may I give the prescription that goes with the salve. I'll read from the label: "To be used several times daily. Do not store! Apply generously over the affected area. If unusual reactions occur, don't be alarmed." Included with the prescription are a number of free samples:

"I'm sorry, Sweetheart."

"I apologize, Dad."

"That's my fault, son."

"Sorry, boss."

"My mistake, sir."

"Forgive me, will you?"

"Excuse me."

"I am sorry!"

By the way, this particular prescription is signed by the Master Physician. I have yet to see any of his remedies fail . . . when we use them.

May I give you my own witness that the words, "I am sorry," really do work. For some of us they are hard to learn to say, but they are well worth saying. I know that a kind heavenly parent would have us use them more often than we do. I know that he lives and that when we sincerely start using those words, we will start to become as he is. May we do so, especially in our homes and with those we say we love.

24

Noble Revenge

Around most golf courses, the story is told of a middle-aged golfer who loved to play the game every day. He had one physical problem that hindered his game. It seemed that his eyesight was failing and he couldn't follow the flight of the ball when he teed off. He mentioned his concern to the golf pro at the club. The pro said: "I can help you with your dilemma. One of our members, who is now well past eighty and can't play any more, still has marvelous eyesight, and I would be happy to send him out with you each time to assist in following the ball."

The arrangements were made and the next day the old-timer was paired with the poor-sighted golfer. On the first tee he hit a tremendous drive that soared into the heavens. He said to his new friend, "Where is it? Where is it?"

The old-timer answered, "I see it! I see it!"

And the golfer said, "Where? Where?"

And the old-timer replied: "I forgot! I forgot!"

It is often thought that, as we get older, it becomes more difficult to remember. I suppose to some degree that's true—names, places, and dates all seem harder to recall. In some ways I think it would be a blessing if we all had poor memories. Consider the advantage of:

—not being able to remember an unkind remark.
—not being able to recall hurt feelings.
—not being able to recount an insult.
—being able to forget being slighted.
—being able to forget being wronged.
—being able to forget injustice.

That isn't an easy order, but it would certainly be more simple than the pain we inflict on ourselves by remembering every hurtful incident.

The spirit of this gift of forgetting was shown by one man during a train trip.

"A passenger on a dining car looked over the luncheon menu. The list included both chicken salad sandwiches and chicken sandwiches. He decided on the chicken salad sandwich but absentmindedly wrote chicken sandwich on the order slip.

"When the waiter brought the chicken sandwich the customer angrily protested. Most waiters would have immediately picked up the order slip and shown the customer that the mistake was his. This waiter didn't.

"Instead, expressing regret at the error, he picked up the chicken sandwich, returned to the kitchen, and a moment later placed the chicken salad sandwich in front of the customer.

"While eating his sandwich the customer picked up the order slip and saw that the mistake had been his. When it came time to pay the check, the man apologized to the waiter and offered to pay for both sandwiches.

"The waiter's response was, 'No, sir. That's perfectly all right. I'm just happy you've forgiven me for being right.' "

Imagine being right and not having to prove it all the time!

Shakespeare said many wise things, but few seem wiser than a remark penned in *Henry VIII*. The bard put it this way, "Heat not a furnace for your foe so hot that it do singe yourself."

That sage advice could save a few scars along the way. How many of us suffer third-degree burns from our own heat? I think we've all heard individuals say on occasion, "Boy, am I burned!" Unfortunately, when people aim their flamethrowers, they inevitably get caught in their own line of fire.

It was Frank Crane who said: "An injury may only grieve us when remembered. The noblest revenge, therefore, is to forget." Think about that. "Forgetful revenge," then, is the only kind of revenge that works. It can heal both the "hurter" and the "hurtee." Let me illustrate. A young mother told this story of her children and the ability to forgive and forget:

"Jane took great care of her things, especially her tricycle. Because we lived on a busy street then, we had avoided buying her a two-wheeled bicycle because of the danger—so at the age of five she was still chugging along the sidewalk with her knees sticking out under the handlebars. Yet because Jane was so careful, always bringing it [the tricycle] into the garage and never letting it get wet or dirty, it still looked like new.

"Then one day a neighbor child left the tricycle behind our pickup truck and a short time later our sixteen-year-old son, armed with a new driver's license, backed out of the driveway in a hurry. The tricycle emerged from the encounter about seven or eight inches high with a steering wheel that permanently faced the back.

"That tricycle had accompanied Jane through three years of happy childhood, and we were not looking forward to telling her about it. We didn't have to—her sisters were eager to give her a full report of the disaster. When we got home from picking Jane up from kindergarten, she ran to the driveway and looked at the wreckage, then fled to her room and closed the door. I almost went in, but hearing her sobs I decided that it would be better to let her cry it out alone. She emerged a short time later, dry-eyed, dressed in play clothes, and ready for lunch.

"About an hour later she visited the ruined tricycle again, and again spent twenty minutes behind a closed door in her bedroom.

"When our sixteen-year-old son, Tracy, got home that night he was apprehensive, to say the least, and he felt even worse when Jane came into the room, saw him there, and immediately fled back to her bedroom to cry again. He didn't know how he could make amends to her—but it turned out it wouldn't be as hard as he thought. Only a few minutes after Jane had left the room she returned and walked right up to Tracy.

" 'It looks like the shrinker got my bike,' she said with a silly smile.

" 'It wasn't the shrinker, Jane. It was me!' Tracy said grimly.

"She didn't even wait for him to ask forgiveness. She just patted his arm and said breezily, 'I know. It's all right, Tracy. You didn't mean to.' He never saw her shed a tear—nobody did. The incident was forgotten.'' (Sharon Elwell, ''What My Daughters Taught Me,'' *Ensign*, April 1980, pp. 72–73.)

The prophet Isaiah put such things into perspective when he said, ''And a little child shall lead them'' (Isaiah 11:6). If children could run the world, we'd be okay. They have the ability to forget, almost instantaneously. It takes adults a little longer, but sometimes, if we persist, even adults can forget.

The story is told of two brothers, convicted of stealing sheep, who were branded on the forehead with the letters *St*, to indicate ''sheep thief.'' The one couldn't bear the stigma, became bitter, and moved away. Eventually he died and was forgotten. The other brother chose a different course. He said, ''I can't run from what I did, so I'll stay here and win back the respect of my neighbors and myself.'' As the years passed, he built a solid reputation for integrity. One day a stranger saw him, now an old man, with the letters on his forehead. He asked a townsman what they signified. ''It happened a long time ago,'' said the villager. ''I've forgotten the particulars, but I think the letters are an abbreviation for 'saint.' ''

Would that we too could forget the particulars. As Lord Herbert observed, ''He that cannot forgive others breaks the bridge over which he must pass himself, for every man has need to be forgiven.''

What a difference it would make in our world if we would seek the revenge of forgetfulness, if we could become such people as:

—parents who would forget that their children lack maturity and would concentrate their efforts on teaching and loving them.

—young people who would forget that their parents aren't perfect and would spend more time supporting them.

—friends who would forget the pettiness that comes as a natural part of mortality and would concentrate on lifting each other.

—family and friends who would concentrate more on things of the heart and less on petty jealousies and material things.

—neighbors who would forget other neighbors' dogs and garbage cans and seek to help, not hinder, each other.

—nations who would forget threats and national pride and would spend their energies in solving their own problems.

That's just a start, but it would be a great step forward.

The example for such a world was given us by the Savior. When we offend him, and truly repent, he offers us what no one else can. He said of our sins, "I, the Lord, remember them no more" (D&C 58:42). No holding grudges; no trying to get even; no attitude problem—only simple forgetfulness.

Let me just say that, as a member of the human race, I know what it is like to sit and conjure up ways to "get even" with those who have offended me, but I also know the sweetness and peace of simply forgetting my hurt feelings. Every time I do I seem to grow stronger. We all do. We enjoy life more fully. Remember: "An injury can only grieve us when remembered. The noblest revenge, therefore, is to forget."

25

Bread and Jam

Have you ever been reading and allowed your mind to wander? I have, and there are times when such wandering proves most rewarding. One night as I was reading and pondering the scriptures, I came upon a verse that caused me to reflect upon my life, my stewardship and contributions: "His lord said unto him, Well done, thou good and faithful servant" (Matthew 25:21).

That particular verse has caused me some concern. I have often wondered—what if the translation of that scripture had read, "Well, Dunn, art thou a good and faithful servant?" Naturally, after reading those words, my mind took flight and I found myself thinking of the circumstances surrounding the time when that appraisal will no doubt be given to each of us. When that hour does arrive, we will have concluded our activities as far as our mortality is concerned. Then at some point we will have the sacred privilege of giving the Lord an accounting of our stewardship. I am certain that even though we left some things undone, there will be praise and acceptance for those things we did accomplish. It seems to me, however, that while we are here in mortality all of us need and could use a spiritual boost in areas where our performance has been acceptable. Wouldn't it seem proper that the Lord would expect us to lift and praise each other now? Must we wait until the end of the journey to receive a word of commendation?

I think we all have seen the results of a sincere compliment. It can be a wonderful thing to witness. I have seen a small boy's face light up as his father put his arm around him, looked intently into his eyes, and said, "Son, that was a great job!" Small boys don't cry easily, but this one almost did. I once saw a father pat his teenage daughter on the back and say, "Honey, if you weren't so cute we wouldn't have boys prowling around here all the time." He smiled and winked, and she beamed. What a marvelous thing to do! What a great joy it is to be recognized! What a difference it makes in our lives to be praised! We even begin to act the way people think we are.

"The story is told of a young psychology student who was serving in the army and who decided to test the following theory. Drawing K.P., he was given the job of passing out apricots at the end of the chow line. If you know the military, you know that apricots are not a sought-after item.

"He asked the first few men that came by, 'You don't want any apricots, do you?' Ninety percent said 'no!'

"Then he tried the positive approach: 'You do want apricots, don't you?' About half answered, 'Uh, yeah, I'll take some.'

"Then he tried a third test based on the fundamental either/or selling technique. This time he
asked, 'One dish of apricots or two?' And in spite of
the fact that soldiers don't like army apricots, 40
percent took two dishes and 50 percent took one!"

I really believe that the way we serve up life makes
a great deal of difference in how we're able to digest
it. We can have a steady diet of negative comments,
sarcastic looks, and critical words, but that does not
do much for life. Or, we can dish up honest, sincere
praise and kindly looks when they are rightly
deserved. We can look for every opportunity to
compliment and lift, and we can make those around
us feel as if they really matter—because they do.

What really worries me is that, while there are
some of us who see opportunities to praise and build,
we often fail to do so because of lack of time or some
other excuse. What a shame! What a lost privilege.
Here's an example:

"A fine old New England gentleman . . . used to
stop by occasionally at an antique shop in New
Hampshire to sell furniture. One day after he left, the
antique dealer's wife said she wished she had told
him how much she enjoyed his visits. The husband
said, 'Next time let's tell him so.' The following
summer a young woman came in and introduced
herself as the daughter of the old gentleman. Her
father, she said, had died. Then the wife told her
about the conversation she and her husband had had
after the father's last visit. The young woman's eyes
filled with tears. 'Oh, how much good that would
have done my father!' she cried. 'He was a man who
needed to be reassured that he was liked.'

" 'Since that day,' the shopkeeper said later,
'whenever I think something particularly nice about a

person, I tell them. I might never get another chance.' '' (*Soundings*, vol. A, no. 1.)

There's the secret—the minute we see an opportunity to say something nice about someone, let's take it! Don't wait. I know we all have made similar mistakes. We say, "Well, I'll do it the next time, or the next day, or next week." But somehow time gets away, and although flowers are nice at the funeral, a compliment to the living is even more beautiful.

Have you ever seen the power of bread and jam? It's always a winner. All you need to do to attract children is to invite them into your home and spread some soft butter and homemade jam on fresh bread. Count Leo Tolstoy knew that secret and passed it on to his small daughter. After the young girl had been treated rudely by a friend, she ran to her father and demanded that he punish the offender immediately. Her father knew just what to do. "If I do that," he explained, "then both you and I would have an enemy. But if you went into the pantry, spread some jam on two pieces of bread, took them outside, and gave one of them to the boy who pushed you down, it would work just like magic to make you friends again. Try it!"

As she stood in the yard slowly eating her bread and jam, she saw the boy watching her. He started coming toward her, then stopped. She held out the bread. He hesitated a minute, then ran toward her and took it. They smiled at each other as they sat down together to enjoy the sweetness of a piece of bread and jam.

Well, that's how praise works. Just hand it out and see how people respond. They will love it! We all need it. (But in giving praise, be certain it is honest and deserved, for nothing is more shallow than praise not earned. Even the recipient knows it is false.) Let's start with those around us—parents, brothers and sisters, sons and daughters, husbands or wives. They may be shocked, but the rewards can never be measured. There is good in everyone and when we look for the positive, it can be found.

During a recent convalescent period I found I had many private and sobering moments that gave me greater insight into how fragile life can be. Emerging from the experience, I have determined that I will become more cognizant of people's goodness and their good deeds. I will try to judge less and compliment more. There is so much we can do to lift, to praise, and to encourage.

The late Donald C. Luce was a great man according to worldly standards, but I believe he was even greater in the sight of God. Among his personal effects was found the following prayer, which undoubtedly explains much of his goodness. As I mature, I see more clearly why it is so:

"Lord, thou knowest better than I know myself that I am growing older and will some day be old. Keep me from the fatal habit of thinking I must say something on every subject and on every occasion. Release me from craving to straighten out everybody's affairs. Make me thoughtful but not moody; helpful but not bossy. With my vast store of wisdom, it seems a pity not to use it all: but thou knowest, Lord, that I want a few friends at the end.

"Keep my mind free from the recital of endless details; give me wings to get to the point. Seal my lips on my aches and pains; they are increasing, and love of rehearsing them is becoming sweeter as the years go by. I dare not ask for grace enough to enjoy the tales of others' pains, but help me to endure them with patience.

"I dare not ask for improved memory, but for a growing humility, and a lessened cocksureness when my memory seems to clash with the memories of others. Teach me the glorious lesson that occasionally I may be mistaken.

"Keep me reasonably sweet. I do not want to be a saint—some of them are so hard to live with: A sour old person is one of the crowning works of the devil. Give me the ability to see the good things in unexpected places and talents in unexpected people, and give me, O Lord, the grace to tell them so." (*Bits & Pieces*, June 1985.)

What a wonderful and worthy goal! I truly believe that giving praise can be enjoyable and extremely worthwhile. Let's develop the habit of seeing the positive traits and the good in our family and fellowman as we prepare ourselves for the day when our Lord and Savior can give to us the greatest compliment of all, "Well done, thou good and faithful servant: . . . enter thou into the joy of thy Lord" (Matthew 25:21).

IV

A Promise of Sunshine:

Reaching for

Eternal Light

26

Just Ask

Emily Dickinson once wrote:

I never saw a moor,
I never saw the sea;
Yet know I how the heather looks,
And what a wave must be.

I never spoke with God,
Nor visited in heaven;
Yet certain am I of the spot
As if the chart were given.

What magnificent certainty this verse expresses—
faith that some in this century must look on with
envy and think of as part of another time, another
age. Many think that we of the last half of the twentieth century have grown beyond certainty, beyond
God. In the place of absolute moral values and rights
and wrongs, we have that rather uncomfortable
sliding scale of relativity that so many embrace. It is

summed up in the sentence, "It's right, if it feels good." And in the place of God, we have ourselves, our own egos, our inflated wills. Where on earth can we find heaven?

My uncle, Paul Roberts, gives us this expression to ponder:

> Does the moon question whom it is serving
> When it brings us its soft, mellow light?
> Does it pause, lest some soul, undeserving,
> May rejoice in the beauty of night?
>
> When the first evening stars are appearing
> And our toil-weary hearts are made glad,
> Does God dim the stars' radiance, fearing
> That a few of those hearts may be bad?
>
> 'Ere he drenches the planet in beauty
> Does he ask us to believe or to care?
> Must we prove our devotion to duty
> 'Ere the father will grant us our share?
>
> If we pause for a moment and ponder
> Such love for the children of men,
> Can we question that somewhere out yonder
> He will give us all beauty again.
>
> Then why conjure a future, unpleasant
> Or despair o'er the path we have trod?
> Let us thrill to the joys of the present
> While we trust the veiled future to God.

A man of the last century might give us some direction here. In the mid-1840s, Henry David Thoreau went to live on the edge of a pond called Walden, not to escape life, but to find it. He had studied man's great thoughts at Harvard University, but he said his classes "taught all the branches, but none of the roots."

"I went to the woods," he explained, "because I wished to live deliberately, to front only the essential facts of life, and to see if I could not learn what it had to teach, and not, when I came to die, discover that I had not lived."

His Walden Pond was only two miles from the center of Concord, Massachusetts, within earshot of the church bells of the little city, but he went there, as he said, to escape the "restless, nervous, bustling trivial nineteenth century," and find out about life's very essence. He considered the ways of worms and waterbugs. He even filled several pages of a book with his observations of a battle between two types of ants—all in an effort to get to some hidden truth about the nature of existence.

Well, we who are part of this restless, nervous, bustling, and sometimes trivial twentieth century may find that we need to retreat from it all ourselves to find the truth. We may not be able to retreat to a physical location to spend twenty-six months on a pond two miles from our city, but we may need to retreat from the skepticism, the materialism, the pressures, and the flimflam to speak with the kind of certainty of truth Emily Dickinson had—"I never spoke with God, / Nor visited in heaven; / Yet certain am I of the spot / As if the chart were given." We want to know God, and know that he knows us, but how do we even begin to do it? How do we get personal revelation to guide us through our days? The Lord has an individual message for each of us—a personalized map of mortality—but too often we choose to travel without it.

Let me tell you the most profound secret about receiving personal revelation for your own life, if you're tired of wandering. It is this: The Lord usually doesn't give us answers we haven't sought. We may often think of him as being like an interfering mother-in-law who's got plenty of unasked-for advice. But that's not the way he operates. In most cases, if we don't ask, he doesn't give us direction. He doesn't come down and zap us with a revelation we haven't been seeking. This is because the Lord cannot reveal himself or his direction for us unless we have made ourselves receptive. A two-way radio can't work if the receiver is turned off.

To understand this further, let's compare the receiving of spiritual direction to the discovery of a new scientific secret. No scientist could hope to solve one of the mysteries of the universe unless he had thoroughly immersed himself in the topic. When a scientist hopes to chart new territory, he studies intently for years, runs countless experiments, compares notes with others, attends conferences, and directs his thoughts continually to the problem at hand. With this concentration, he has much greater opportunity to come upon the solution to his problem than has the man on the street who didn't even know there was a problem.

In fact, we have marvelous stories of scientific discovery in which a man or woman, after years of effort, suddenly has the solution to a scientific puzzle arrive in the mind wholly by inspiration, long before scientific data made the answer evident. In the field of chemistry, the best example is that of Freidrich August Kekule, professor of chemistry at Ghent, who, for some time, had been puzzling over the structure of a compound called benzene. Several competing theories of this structure existed but none was entirely satisfactory. Then one afternoon he fell asleep and dreamed he saw atoms in long rows, twisting and twining like snakes. He then reported,

"But look! What was that? One of the snakes had seized hold of its own tail and the form whirled mockingly before my eyes. As if by a flash of lightning I awoke. . . ." His dream had given him the answer to the structure of benzene, a structure that was later confirmed by research. Benzene is the foundation of many of the vast chemical developments which have transformed society today.

Now, would this inspiration have come to Kekule if he had not been diligently seeking for the structure of benzene? And even if it had come, would he have been able to interpret its meaning if he hadn't first asked the question? Of course not! Answers don't make sense without the questions that accompany them.

In scripture there is a record of a prophet named Enos who went into the forest to pray to the Lord and seek the knowledge that he had been forgiven of his sins. He asked the Lord, all right—our prime prerequisite for receiving revelation. But his was no casual, off-the-cuff asking. He says of it, "And my soul hungered; and I kneeled down before my Maker, and I cried unto him in mighty prayer and supplication for mine own soul; and all the day long did I cry unto him; yea, and when the night came I did still raise my voice high that it reached the heavens" (Enos 1:4). It was only after this wrenching, enervating struggle that the Lord answered him with a sure, strong voice, saying, "Enos, thy sins are forgiven thee, and thou shalt be blessed" (Enos 1:5).

He got the answer because he asked, and only because he asked. Like Kekule, the scientist, he immersed himself in the problem at hand—receiving revelation. We can only imagine with the hours involved in that prayer that he was considering closely why he needed revelation, what it meant to him; evaluating his expectations of the Lord; and with every hour his understanding was enhanced. He was becoming a person more able to recognize and receive revelation when it came. Those hours in prayer weren't for the Lord, they were for him.

Receiving revelation is like any other magnificent achievement. It comes only because someone asks and because someone cares enough to really study and learn and try. Revelation is available for every human being, but it is not free. Its price is that a person be prepared to hear because he first asked.

Thoreau retreated from his society for two years to find his version of truth. Since we can't always do that, let's at least retreat from our personal hubbub long enough to ask how to live with it gracefully when we are back in its clutches. That we may do so, knowing with assurance where heaven is as if a map were given, is my desire for us all.

27

You Stand Tallest
When You Kneel
to Pray

Do you ever get the feeling that you've grown beyond the need for God—that you don't need to talk to him today or this month or this year, because like the little red hen in the children's nursery story, you can do it all yourself? The world would certainly have you believe that this is so. Everywhere we turn we see marks of man's marvelous independence. We have knowledge that penetrates the secrets of space, know-how to recombine the very elements of life, and little opportunity to test our strengths in a world that so easily supplies our survival needs. All this can lull us into the false security, the heady belief that we can go it alone in life.

For all of us, being human, as surely as the stars come out at night, there will come a day when life deals roughly with us, when the battle is too fierce, when the wall is insurmountable, when the darkness is too deep to go on with our own little light. There will come a day when you will have a longing that seems to wring your very soul, and in that day there will be only one person to whom you can really turn to find help—your Father in Heaven.

You will face the time when you will need to know the Lord, not as someone distant out in space, but as your own best friend who is with you wherever you are, whatever you do. Do you know him this way?

Most of us like to think we know our Heavenly Father, but too often I hear people say to me that their prayers somehow fall short, without power to lift into his presence. They wonder, as have scholars and saints through the centuries, what it is to really pray —what it means to get beyond stilted words, hurried phrases, rushed repetitions. How many thousands of us have asked ourselves the question, "Do I really talk to Him when I kneel to pray?"

As I pondered these thoughts, the flashing lights of an ambulance rushed down a nearby residential street and stopped before the home of a newlywed couple. The young man, in his early twenties, had mysteriously stopped breathing. As the paramedics connected him to an oxygen supply, his young bride was whispering under her breath, "Dear God, let him breathe; let him breathe; make him breathe." Here were no fancy words, but here was a prayer that connected. The young man began to breathe on his own and a sweet spirit of assurance filled the room. We can learn something from the prayer of this young woman. The power of prayer is not found in its eloquence or its posturing. The power of prayer is in its simplicity, in its sincerity.

Perhaps that is why children have a way of defining and understanding prayer. Just consider the following quotations from a group of five-year-olds. Their definitions come pretty close to home.

THE CHURCH OF JESUS CHRIST
OF LATTER-DAY SAINTS

Plymouth 2nd Ward - Sacrament Meeting
November 18, 1990

"And ye shall go forth in the power of my Spirit,
preaching my gospel, two by two, in my name, lifting up
your voices as with the sound of a trump, declaring
my word like unto angels of God".   D&C 42:6

Opening Hymn #93	"Prayer of Thanksgiving"
Invocation	Donna Dobozenski
Sacrament Hymn #193	"I Stand All Amazed"
Administered by	Aaronic Priesthood
Speaker	Randy Sarles
Testimonies	Jack & Gunnel Ostvig
Primary Children	"I Am A Child of God"
Concluding Speaker	Jay Ostvig
Closing Hymn #270	"I'll Go Where You Want Me To Go"
Benediction	Tex Ostvig

Choir practice every Sunday noon in chapel.

Nov. 18 - STAKE CHOIR rehearsal tonight at 7:30 p.m. in
Bloomington for the STAKE CHRISTMAS CONCERT: "The Music
of Christmas" will be performed Sun. Dec 9 at Stake Center.
This will be a joyful holiday musical experience for all
members and their guests. The Choir is under direction of
Marietta Fossum. All interested invited to sing w. choir.

Nov. 18 - Missionary Farewell Open House for Jay Ostvig
at the Ostvig home: 4718 Hampton Rd. Mound from 2-6PM.

Dec. 2 - All members of the Church are cordially invited
to participate in the First Presidency Christmas Devotional.
This program will originate in the Tabernacle on Temple
Square on 2 Dec at 6 p.m. MST. It will be broadcast live
over the Church satellite network at 7 p.m. Minnesota time.
This is intended for the entire family and will include
Christmas messages from the First Presidency and music by
the Tabernacle Choir.

Brother Ewing

"Prayer is to close your eyes and think."

"Prayer is to bow your head and close your eyes while someone else talks."

"Prayer is when you quietly yell for Heavenly Father to help you."

"Prayer is to tell Heavenly Father that you are afraid and wait while he protects you."

"Prayer is to ask him to help you do something that you think you can't do."

"Prayer is the talking we do when we are almost asleep."

Prayer is not meant to impress the Lord, to add up Brownie points in some invisible book in heaven. When he commanded us to "pray always," it wasn't for him; it wasn't because he relishes the sight of us bowing before him like idol worshipers. It was because he knew how desperately we would need his help in this mortal journey, that we would at times be frantic in our pleas, saying, "Lead me, guide me, walk beside me. Help me find the way."

If you pray and are dissatisfied, perhaps it is because you have learned to use someone else's words; perhaps you are content to throw out generalities that are not sincerely from your heart. A prayer, after all, should be the most honest form of conversation, when with simplicity you tell the Lord quite directly how it feels to be you. You cannot be too specific in your prayers. Say, "Today, I did this, and I felt that, and I needed your help when this hurt me or scared me or made me mad." With him there is no need for false fronts, for he sees you as you are.

James Montgomery wrote:

> Prayer is the soul's sincere desire,
> Uttered or unexpressed,
> The motion of a hidden fire
> That trembles in the breast.

Prayer is the burden of a sigh,
The falling of a tear,
The upward glancing of an eye
When none but God is near.

Prayer is the simplest form of speech
That infant lips can try;
Prayer, the sublimest strains that reach
The Majesty on high.

Prayer is the Christian's vital breath,
The Christian's native air,
His watchword at the gates of death;
He enters heaven with prayer.
(*Hymns*, 1985, no. 145.)

Today there is a great deal of talk about how to pray and where to pray and what time to pray. There are those who believe that the formula is everything. But I have learned that although there may be many ways to pray, the divine principle does not change. It is said that French sailors utter these words as a prayer: "Dear Lord, thou art so great and my ship is so small." The prayer ends there—there is no more. But in that brief expression is tied the unchanging divine principle behind prayer, the recognition that pierces beyond intellect and words into the very bone marrow of your body, the understanding that you are utterly dependent upon the Lord for every good thing, that he alone is the very font of love and goodness and light in the entire universe.

If you want to pray, talk from your heart as you would talk to your own father, however informal your words. The following verse illustrates the point:

"The proper way for a man to pray,"
  Said deacon Lemuel Keys,
"And the only proper attitude,
  Is down upon his knees."

"No, I should say the way to pray,"
  Said Reverend Dr. Wise,
"Is standing straight with outstretched arms
  And rapt and upturned eyes."

"Oh, no, no, no," said Elder Snow;
  "Such posture is too proud.
A man should pray with eyes fast closed,
  And head contritely bowed."

"It seems to me his hands should be
  Austerely clasped in front,
With both thumbs pointed toward the ground,"
  Said Reverend Dr. Hunt.

"Last year, I fell in Hodgskin's well,
  Head first," said Cyrus Brown.
"With both my heels a-striking up,
  My head a-pointin' down."

"And I made a prayer right then and there;
  Best prayer I ever said . . .
The prayin'est prayer I ever prayed,
  A-standin' on my head."

Our prayers are only as powerful as they are earnest. Mere words do not suffice. Mormon, an ancient prophet, said, "Pray unto the Father with all the energy of heart" (Moroni 7:48). I've discovered that to have that kind of energy, that kind of soul strength, we need to somehow break beyond the confines of self, to begin to realize, however dimly at first, how great and glorious is our Father, how totally he loves us, how personally he knows us. Remember, he can call you by name.

In the Bible we read, "The eyes of the Lord are upon the righteous, and his ears are open unto their cry" (Psalm 34:15). And God promises not only to hear our prayers but to answer them as well: "Thou shalt call, and I will answer thee. . . ." (Job 14:15).

The scriptures are full of answers to prayer. Abraham's servant prays and Rebekah appears; Jacob wrestles and prays, and Esau's mind is turned from revenge to understanding; Moses prays, and the Red Sea divides, Isaiah prays, and a dream is revealed; Daniel prays, and the lions are tamed; Nehemiah starts a prayer, and the king's heart is softened in a minute; Elijah prays, and a drought of several years ends; Nephi prays, and the Lord directs; Enos prays, and his sins are forgiven; Peter prays, and he receives a vision; Paul prays, and he is directed to Ananias; Joseph Smith prays, and God the Father and his Son appear.

In view of such overwhelming evidence of the powers of prayer, how can anyone question? Yet it is common for people to complain that they have received no answer to their prayers.

Randolph Ayre tells of a man who was hard pressed for money. He prayed fervently to the Lord, asking for riches. "The Lord, hearing the prayer coming up from earth, called one of his angels and said, 'That poor fellow needs money. Send some down to him.' The angel left to fulfill the assignment but returned some time later and said:

" 'Lord, I have looked over the vaults of heaven and can find no money. We have only that which "neither moth nor rust doth corrupt, and where thieves do not break through nor steal." But while we have no money, we have some wonderful ideas and insights. Shall we send some of those down to him?'

"The man continued to pray and showed great faith and the Lord was delighted and said, 'Yes, open the windows of heaven and pour out so many insights and ideas that he will have more than he needs.'

''The Lord showered wealth upon this man—not a hail of coins which might be injurious to him, but rather insight and ideas which, through work and diligence, could be transformed into the needed money.'' (J. Randolph Ayre, *Illustrations to Inspire* [Salt Lake City: Bookcraft, 1968], pp. 16–17.)

I wonder if that man, who seems to have been earnest enough in prayer, though some might say a little shallow, could even begin to understand what a great blessing he had received in the Lord's answer. Perhaps the reason we don't pray as often as we should, or at all, is because we, too, lack understanding of how the Lord helps us.

We find lots of obstacles to prayer. Let's look at two of the big ones.

First, many of us believe we're not good enough to pray. We simply can't imagine that the Lord could be interested in our little concerns. We believe that our imperfect state forever bars us from communication with the very author of the universe. If we pray at all, we keep our prayers general and short, and very impersonal. Either our real or imagined imperfect state stops us cold. I think when we feel like this we are suffering from a Huckleberry Finn syndrome. Do you remember Huck? Recall with me his experience with prayer:

''I about made up my mind to pray, and see if I couldn't try to quit being the kind of boy I was and be better. So I kneeled down. But the words wouldn't come. Why wouldn't they? It warn't no use to try and hide it from Him. . . . I knowed very well why they wouldn't come. It was because my heart warn't right; it was because I warn't square; it was because I was playing double. I was letting *on* to give up sin, but away inside of me I was holding on to the biggest one of all. I was trying to make my mouth *say* I would do the right thing and the clean thing, . . . but deep down in me I knowed it was a lie, and He knowed it. You can't pray a lie—I found that out." (Mark Twain, *The Adventures of Huckleberry Finn* [New York: The New American Library, Inc., n.d.], pp. 208–9.)

For those of us who suffer from the Huck Finn syndrome, it is time to really learn that our circumstances, our weaknesses, are not paramount to the Lord. He is willing and able to take us as we are and make us what we can become—what he knows we can become. All we have to do is to give him our hearts, riddled with sin and weaknesses as they may be.

It is when we are most caught up with our own shortcomings that we most need to pray. The Nephite prophet Jacob reminded us that God sees things as they really are, and things as they really will be (see Jacob 4:13). We don't! To become what we were meant to be we have to tap that precious perspective and learn what hidden glories lie in our hearts.

The second great obstacle to prayer is pride. We hate somehow to admit that we are not entirely self-sufficient. We sometimes have difficulty admitting there are rules for living outside our own. We are loath to admit even to ourselves that for our very breath we are dependent on a higher power. Yet down deep there is a divine spark that causes us all to seek.

I remember so well several times during the war when men old enough to be my father were trying desperately to get me to compromise gospel standards. They were proud men with high rank and position. My religious beliefs often only caused them to try harder to make me commit a wrong.

Interestingly enough, when these things occurred, I found that if I kept diligently to my principles, these same men eventually came to respect me, and some even changed. One such experience took place after many months of training, when the time came for us to face our first combat encounter. One big, burly sergeant, who was my platoon leader, crawled into my foxhole shortly after the enemy had overrun our position and with a quivering voice said: "Dunn, you know God. Will you help me find him?"

It's been said that you stand tallest when you kneel to pray. An examination of the lives of the world's greatest people bears out that truth. Maybe that is because the movers and motivators of our world—those who stand at the very pinnacle of intellect and power—can see most clearly, as they view the wide expanse of mankind, how frail we really are, how little control we hold over our destinies without the Lord's help.

One of the most famous paintings of the father of our country, George Washington, depicts him on his knees at Valley Forge during the bleak winter of 1777 when the colonial forces were almost defeated by the cold; shortages of food, clothing, and military supplies; and low morale. Mason L. Weems, biographer of Washington, wrote:

"In the winter of '77 while Washington, with the American army, lay encamped at Valley Forge, [a Quaker] had occasion to pass through the woods near headquarters. Treading in his way along the venerable grove, suddenly he heard the sound of a human voice, which, as he advanced, . . . at length became like the voice of one speaking much in earnest. As he approached the spot with cautious step, whom should he behold, in a dark natural bower of ancient oaks, but the commander in chief of the American armies on his knees at prayer! Motionless with surprise, [the onlooker] continued on the place till the general, having ended his devotions, arose; and with a countenance of angelic serenity, retired to headquarters. [The Quaker who had viewed this incident went home and said to his wife that he had seen Washington in earnest prayer.] 'If George Washington be not a man of God,' [he said] 'I am greatly deceived—and still more shall I be deceived, if God do not, through him, work out a great salvation for America.' " (Mason Weems, *A History of the Life and Death Virtues and Exploits of General George Washington* [n.p.: Macy–Masius Publishers, 1927], pp. 300–301.)

President Abraham Lincoln sought our Heavenly Father when he had difficulties and needed divine guidance. Here is an example from his life:

"[General Sickles had noticed that before the portentous battle of Gettysburg, upon the result of which perhaps hung the fate of the nation, President Lincoln was apparently free from the oppressive care which frequently weighed him down. After it was all past, the general asked Lincoln how that was.] Mr. Lincoln hesitated, but finally replied: 'Well, I will tell you how it was. In the pinch of your campaign up there, when everybody seemed panic-stricken and nobody could tell what was going to happen, oppressed by the gravity of our affairs, I went to my room one day and locked the door and got down on my knees before Almighty God and prayed to him mightily for victory at Gettysburg. I told Him that this war was His, and our cause His cause, but we could not stand another Fredericksburg or Chancellorsville. Then and there I made a solemn vow to Almighty God that if He would stand by our boys at Gettysburg, I would stand by him. . . . And after that, I don't know how it was, and I cannot explain it, soon a sweet comfort crept into my soul. The feeling came that God had taken the whole business into His own hands, and that things would go right at Gettysburg, and that is why I had no fears about you.' '' (John Wesley Hill, *Abraham Lincoln: Man of God* [New York: G. P. Putnam's Sons, 1920], pp. 339–40.)

On another occasion President Lincoln said: ''I have been driven to my knees over and over again because I have nowhere else to go'' (Hill, pp. 331–32).

Instances of prayer giving strength are not limited to decades ago. Many of us can testify today that on numerous occasions prayers were our rallying point.

Isn't that what we all need, desperately—the Lord's strength and love? Not just to face those times when the scaffolding of our world comes shattering around our feet, but to face our every day. A higher hand can and will enter our case. The Lord has asked us that in everything, by prayer, we let our requests be made known unto him. We learn that we should ''cry unto him for mercy; for he is mighty to save. . . . Cry unto him when ye are in your fields, yea, over all your flocks. Cry unto him in your houses, yea, over all your household, both morning, midday, and evening. Yea, cry unto him against the power of your enemies. . . . Cry unto him over the crops of your fields, that ye may prosper in them. . . . But this is not all; ye must pour out your souls in your closets, and your secret places, and in your wilderness.'' (Alma 34:18–26.)

Pour out your soul to him who is your God. It is not so hard to do. Cry out, ''Father,'' and he will be there. I give my personal witness that this is so.

28

Carry an Umbrella

James Russell Lowell once remarked, "Children are God's apostles, sent forth, day by day, to preach of love, and hope, and peace." It is no wonder, since they are so fresh from God's presence. They are so open and trusting that sometimes it is almost frightening. It was the Lord who said, "Verily I say unto you, Except ye be converted, and become as little children, ye shall not enter into the kingdom of heaven" (Matthew 18:3).

I thought of that scripture in Matthew as I read a wonderful story told by Maggie Porter. The incident took place many years ago when she was a very young girl. She was without a father, and her mother was seriously ill. She wrote:

"My dear mother was ill. She had been, for days, unable to eat anything. It grieved me very much. I wanted always to see her well and happy. When she was depressed, I was depressed also. When she was sad, I, too, was sad. This was a lonely Sunday. No churches or Sunday Schools to attend. I had never been inside of a Sunday School. It was about time for dinner. Mother seemed a little better that day and I was so glad. I went to her room and asked her what she would like to eat.

" 'Well, dear,' she answered, 'I don't have much choice. If I eat, I will have to eat just what is on hand.'

"At this time we did not have much of anything left in the cellar except tomatoes; she told me that she would rather have anything else, if she could have it. She thought a moment, then said, 'If I could really have what I want most, it would be some good cold peaches fresh from the cellar.' Then she laughed as she added, 'I guess I'll just try to imagine the tomatoes are big, juicy peaches and let it go at that.'

"The cellar was under Mother's prayer room over at the bunkhouse. I well remember how hot it was and what a temptation it was to linger there in the cool dark cellar when I was sent for things. Sometimes I was scolded for taking so much time on these errands.

"Before going to the cellar, however, I made my way into the little back bedroom where I was born—the room my mother always used to go to for prayer. I knelt beside the bed and told the Lord in my own simple way what a wonderful mother I had and how I wanted to bring her some peaches for her dinner. I arose happy in the trusted faith, or shall I say knowledge, that my prayer had been answered. I walked into the cellar and lighted the candle so that I might be able to see better. There was one opened tomato case sitting on top of a full case. With great effort I lifted off the top box. I took a hammer that was lying on the table and with much lifting and banging I tore loose the board from the unopened case, then lifted out another can from the bottom layer. I ran back to the house. I knew that inside the can I carried, with the red tomato picture on it, would be luscious yellow peaches. I rushed in all excited. 'Mother,' I cried, 'I've got your peaches.'

'' 'It looks very much like tomatoes to me,' added Aunt Laura Tolman. Aunt Laura was our hired girl at the time.

'' 'I don't care what the picture says,' I assured them. 'These are peaches!'

'' 'Bless your heart,' Mother added. 'We'll imagine they're peaches and eat them anyway.'

"I rushed for the can cutter. I jabbed the blade into the can and golden peach juice oozed out. I took my finger and tasted it. 'Oh, Mother, the Lord did hear my prayer,' I cried. 'They are peaches.'

"When I carried a big dish of the golden fruit to her bed with some toast, she took me in her arms and wept and asked me what I did to get peaches. I told her of my prayer and my effort to lift the heavy case and open the other one, and how I discarded the first can and took the second one.

"After I left the room, Aunt Laura said, 'Well, they just made a mistake when they labeled the cans. Isn't it strange it should happen just that way?'

"Mother said to her, 'Yes, it's strange, in all my life I never found peaches in tomato cans; and that she should open another case and select a certain can. I know the Lord answered her prayers and guided her hand to that one can, and don't try to tell me differently.'

"I slowly pondered the situation as I went leisurely back across the street to our prayer room and thanked the Lord for answering my prayer."

What a remarkable young lady! And what remarkable faith!

I have often sat and pondered the amount of faith I have as a husband and father—as a child of God. As I have done so, this thought has occurred to me: How many blessings do we deny ourselves because we are not in a position to receive them? In other words, how is our faith?

The Apostle Paul indicated that faith is "the substance of things hoped for, the evidence of things not seen" (Hebrews 11:1). In light of that understanding, how do we get in a position so that we can be filled with that assurance from the Lord?

To illustrate, let me share another account of faith that took place during World War II. I admit that my own experience during that war makes this story a very special one.

"We were only one Berlin subway stop away from home when the air-raid sirens began wailing. From past experience, we knew we had a little over five minutes before the bombers would arrive and I waited tensely, feeling the increasing anxiety of my three sisters, Edith, Esther, and Ursula, as we all tried mentally to make the subway move faster. Fortunately, Mother was there. Her mere presence kept panic at bay, but she moved quickly too, when we reached our stop, shepherding us out on the platform.

"She had to shout to be heard over the sirens: 'Run, girls! We can get home before the bombs hit!'' She started running with us, then stopped, smiled, and said, 'Don't worry.'

"Frenzied, we shouted, 'Mother, hurry!'

" 'It's all right,' she said. 'We don't need to run. Suddenly, I know where the bombs will fall tonight, and we will be untouched.' Then, she pointed out the places the bombs would hit and walked unhurriedly along with us. We were still nervous, but the serenity of her faith was contagious. And by the time we reached home, we had seen the bombers go overhead, heard the bombs burst, and seen the fires begin in the locations she had pointed out." (Personal account told by Karola Hilbert.)

Personally, I don't believe for a minute that the Lord would have given the reward to this good mother's faith if she hadn't first done her part. It was after she ran that the Lord gave her understanding and courage to know what to do. That's a great lesson. Abraham Lincoln said the same thing in these words, "Let us have faith that right makes might, and in that faith let us to the end dare to do our duty as we understand it." The Apostle James said it just a little differently: "Even so faith, if it hath not works, is dead, being alone" (James 2:17).

So, let's pray and fast and exert all our spiritual capacity to bring about the desired faith. But, in the meantime, let's do our part.

I have long appreciated William Lund's classic example of faith plus works:

"Once there was a little girl who took an umbrella to church and it brought about a miracle. It happened in a farming country when there was a drouth. Unless rain came soon, the crops would be lost. So the minister sent out word for everybody to come to the church, please, the next Sunday. Because all together they were going to pray for rain.

"Sunday came, and the streaming sun burned eternally and hotly down. Along the roads, the farmers came driving to church; along the sidewalks the townsfolk were walking to the meeting.

"Every pew was filled. The minister read to them about miracles, so many of them and so beautiful. And then they prayed. People who had never prayed before sent up a cry from their hearts, 'Send the rain, O God, send the rain!'

"And after a bit the church began to grow darker and then the sound of thunder was heard. And finally came the most lovely sound in all the world. It rained and kept on raining. But nobody had brought an umbrella, except one little girl. She had, and there she stood—the only little grain of mustard seed in the midst of unbelief."

As you and I work to have the faith to bring our umbrellas, we'll soon learn what all faithful people have learned—you can't have faith and doubt at the same time. Remember, doubt is the culprit.

I'm reminded of the golfer who had a tough shot from deep in the rough to the green. Secluded from his partners, he knelt down and asked the Lord to bless his shot that it might make it safely to the green. With that prayer, he took a terrific swing. The ball hit a tree and flew into a nearby pond of water. After uttering several interesting words, the golfer looked up to heaven and shouted, "I *knew* it wouldn't work!"

I submit that such an action was not one of faith.

We bring our umbrellas with us in simple ways. Let me suggest a few:

—we need a job—and then we go look for one until we find it.

—we want more money—and then we get some more training to earn it.

—we want more happiness at home—and then we shape up our own lives to help bring it about.

—we need more faith—and so we begin studying the scriptures and praying to understand how to achieve it.

The list goes on, but it must contain two important ingredients: (1) That which we seek must be good and have righteous purpose, and (2) we must omit doubt and believe that the desired results are possible.

Our Father knows what we need. But he also waits for us to have the faith to ask and to actively seek. I am convinced by my own experience that the Lord has blessings unmeasured available to us if we would only take them. He wants us to!

May we seek his spirit and use our faith in bringing to pass our righteous desires.

29

Ready or Not

Some years ago when Michigan State [University] played UCLA, the score was tied at 14 with only seconds left to play. Duffy Daugherty, Michigan State's coach, sent in place kicker Dave Kaiser, who booted a field goal that won the game.

"When [Kaiser] returned to the bench, Daugherty said, 'Nice going, but you didn't watch the ball after you kicked it.'

" 'That's right, Coach,' Kaiser replied. 'I was watching the referee instead to see how he'd signal it. I forgot my contact lenses, and I couldn't see the goal posts.' "

That little anecdote makes a lot of sense. Whenever I think about it I find myself cheering for such action. Those of us who have participated in sports have learned some of life's great lessons. In fact, there are many similarities between life and athletic competition. It seems to me that sometimes, whether we are totally prepared or not, we simply kick the

ball. Contact lenses notwithstanding, helmet un-
buckled, kicking or missing, ready or not, there
comes a time when we ''go for it.'' There can only be
so much practice; there can only be so many time-
outs; there can only be so much time to think—then
there comes the time to act. Good athletes have the
faith and belief that they can perform, but it is never
known until they act.

The Apostle James said:

''What doth it profit, my brethren, though a man
say he hath faith, and have not works? can faith save
him?

''If a brother or sister be naked, and destitute of
daily food,

''And one of you say unto them, Depart in peace,
be ye warmed and filled; notwithstanding ye give
them not those things which are needful to the body;
what doth it profit?

''Even so faith, if it hath not works, is dead, being
alone.

''Yea, a man may say, Thou hast faith, and I have
works: shew me thy faith without thy works, and I
will shew thee my faith by my works.'' (James
2:14–18.)

Now, that's just good sense. We can talk all we
want about heavenly things; we can speculate about
what it will be like to be in the presence of a kind,
wise Heavenly Father and his Son, Jesus Christ; but
talking won't get us there. Planning alone won't do
it, and studying alone won't do it. Sooner or later,
ready or not, we will have to do something about it.
We are going to have to kick the ball whether our
contact lenses are in or not.

I know a young man who learned this lesson in a
most graphic way. His story illustrates what must
happen in our lives if we are to do what needs to be
done.

"[An exhibit at the World's Fair] made a profound impression on me which I shall always remember. There was a man standing on a platform holding an ordinary 2" x 4" board in his hands. His assistant pulled a lever which caused a tremendous amount of electricity to flow into the man's body. The power of the electricity was so great that the board almost instantly caught fire. The man, however, was unharmed.

"He stepped off the platform and proceeded to describe to the audience exactly what had happened and why. After a brief but clear explanation, he asked if everyone understood; were there any questions? Everyone understood; there were no questions.

"Next the man asked how many in the group thought that they could do the same thing? Immediately everyone's hand shot up. The man enthusiastically reached for another board and said, 'All right, who's first?' All was still and very silent. The man looked disappointed. He set the board down, paused for a moment, and then made an analogy which I'll never forget.

"He said, 'The overwhelming majority of the so-called Christian world today have the same kind of faith in God as you have had in this experiment. They believe in God. They believe he created the world. They believe he is all-powerful. They believe he hears and answers prayers. They believe in all these things and many more, but, like you here with this experiment, their belief is vain because they do nothing about it. I ask you, is this faith? No! *Faith is more than intellectual assent.* True faith leads to works. There is not true faith without works.' I silently nodded approval." (Albert Mitchell, *Improvement Era.*)

I add my own nod of approval. There is no true faith without works.

I have met people who desire—and I might add

"righteously"—to do the right thing, but they hesitate to do anything until they feel God has approved. They wait and worry and wait . . . and wait. I understand how they feel. We would all like the continual spiritual guidance of a loving Father in all that we do, but the Lord gives us our agency and expects us to use it. If we really try, the Lord will guide our efforts, but if we open the cupboard door in the morning and expect the Holy Ghost to reveal which cereal to take out, we may be found later on the floor in need of nourishment.

We must act on our own. Certainly, we must obtain all the facts we can. It is important to weigh the evidence and then pray about it. But then, I believe with all my heart, we must act. We must do our very best, but we must act!

Glen Cunningham, America's marvelous Olympic track star and four-time gold medal winner, faced real tragedy as a young boy, but his great faith and works made the difference.

"As a young boy, Glen and his family lived one-half hour closer to the community school house than any of the other families with school children. As a result, Glen and his older brother, Floyd, were given the responsibility of coming early to school during cold weather so they could get the fire going well in the school house before the teacher and the rest of the students arrived.

"One morning, however, a mistake was made in the delivery of fuel for the stove. Instead of kerosene, gasoline was accidentally left at the school. The deliveryman realized the mistake toward the end of his deliveries and raced as fast as he could back to the school, hoping to get there in time to avoid a catastrophe. Sadly, the explosion had already occurred by the time he arrived. The school was destroyed, Floyd was gone; and Glen was terribly burned, especially on his legs. The doctor who attended Glen felt confident of his survival, but told his parents that Glen's legs were too badly burned and would have to be amputated. Martha Cunningham, Glen's mother, refused staunchly to permit the operation, and her will finally prevailed.

"It was a full year afterward when Glen was finally well enough to receive his first set of crutches. They were brought by the doctor who told his mother that Glen would need them all his life. The bandages had come off his legs a month before to reveal a ghastly sight. Both legs had been seared to the bone; the right leg was crooked, 2½ inches short, and pulled up to the knee by the contracted tissue; all five toes and the arch on the left foot were gone. Medically speaking, Glen was clearly disabled for life.

But he overheard the doctor telling his mother these things, and after the doctor left, Glen asked his mother to read the verse from Isaiah 40:31. This was his mother's favorite passage of scripture. It was one that his father had read to the family on the morning of that terrible fire before the boys went to school. It reads: 'But they that wait upon the Lord shall renew their strength; they shall mount up with wings as eagles; they shall run, and not be weary; and they shall walk, and not faint.'

"After Mrs. Cunningham read the verse, Glen responded, 'That verse was meant for me, Mother. I am going to wait upon the Lord to renew my strength, and Mother, I will walk again without these crutches. I'll run and not be weary. The Lord will help me.'

"Following this magnificent expression of faith, Glen put his words into action. His doctor had suggested an hour of leg massages per day. Glen asked if they couldn't be extended longer, reasoning that if an hour would help, longer periods would help more. With his doctor's consent, the massages were extended to as long as four hours a day. For four years this continued until Glen threw his crutches away and he could hobble about. Eventually he began to run, much to his parents' and doctor's delight. Two years later, he was playing tag and baseball. His text from Isaiah decided his life and his career. In 1930 he broke the world interscholastic record in the mile run, finishing in 4.27.7. His victories in the 1936 Olympics are legend.''

There is no question but that the Lord could have healed Glen immediately but he didn't—and, just as important, Glen didn't wait for him to do so. Ready or not, this marvelous young man put works with his faith, and that, together with the blessing of his Heavenly Father, worked a miracle. Remember, God does not cause adversity, but he does allow it, and through adversity we are tested and are able to grow and develop.

I wonder how many of our problems could be eliminated by our own works. Imagine what we could accomplish if we decided to do our very best to overcome them, while at the same time relying on the Lord for his extra strength. I am reminded of ''an old farmer who had plowed around a large rock in one of his fields for years. He had broken several plowshares and a cultivator on it and had grown rather morbid about the rock.

''After breaking another plowshare one day, and remembering all the trouble the rock had caused him through the years, he finally determined to do something about it.

''When he put his crowbar under the rock, he was surprised to discover that it was only about six inches thick and that he could break it up easily. As he was carting it away he had to smile, remembering all the trouble that the rock had caused him and how easy it would have been to get rid of it in the first place."

I believe that all of us by ourselves could carry away many of our "rocks" by just grabbing the crowbar and lifting up. Also, I know from personal experience that we can only lift so far by ourselves, but if we couple our efforts with those of others, and with the help of the Lord, all things are possible.

May we continue to learn to do all we can to be ready, call upon the Lord, and then act.

30

God and Logic

My mother used to wonder when I was a boy if I would someday make a good lawyer. I always enjoyed a good argument on the ball field. If I remember correctly, my comments to the umpires were gems of brilliant logic. But, as a good friend of mine often points out, "There's logic and then there's logic!" In other words, sound logic is wonderful; faulty logic can be disastrous. I recall reading some logic of the second category wherein it was reported that "38,530,460 Americans applied for fishing licenses last year. Only 1,926,523 applied for a marriage license. This proves that fishing is twenty times more popular than marriage!" While I find the logic of that statement humorous, I doubt seriously if it would stand up in court.

It is about another kind of faulty logic, however, that I am currently concerned. As I travel about and talk to good people everywhere, I hear some espouse a belief that is not only illogical but could be harmful.

If you can recall the 1940s and 1950s, or even more recently, you might remember with me the "God is dead" fad. For whatever reasons, some decided to put an end to a belief in a supreme being. Their logic was simple: There is no way to prove he exists; hence, he is dead. Besides, they argue, what kind of a God would allow the world to languish in the blood and horror we inflict on each other? What kind of God would permit the human suffering we see everywhere? Perhaps no single problem has so bothered mankind as the problem of evil in the world. And because evil is so plentiful, it has led many to take the position that "God is dead." To believe otherwise, such thinkers seem to require some physical evidence or a sign. Alma records that there are those whose beliefs or logic are tied to a sign: "Yea, there are many who do say: If thou wilt show unto us a sign from heaven, then we shall know of a surety; then we shall believe" (Alma 32:17).

Now, let me first ask a few questions for you to consider as you think about such reasoning:

What makes a light bulb give light? Electricity, you say. What is electricity?

By the way, what is light? Who invented the eyes to see light?

A bird will migrate from Canada to Argentina. How does it know what course to take or what speed to fly, and why must it do this?

A salmon will swim upstream to have its young. It will jump up fish ladders to return to its origin—then die. Why?

Why does the earth spin at a given speed without ever slowing up so that we have day and night? Who tilts it so that we get the seasons?

The human heart will beat for seventy or eighty years without faltering. How does it get sufficient rest between beats? A kidney will filter poison from the blood and leave only good ingredients. How does it know one from the other?

What power or process prompts the female reproductive organ, once fertilized, to split the tiny ovum until, in time, a baby has the proper number of fingers, eyes, and toes in the right places, and then comes into the world when it is strong enough to live independently?

That last question is one to really ponder. What is behind it all? Is there really something or someone responsible for the order of our existence?

In my life and experience I have learned that there are four different ways one can seek truth: first, by accepting an idea on the authority of someone else; second, by personal experience; third, by reasoning; and fourth, by inspiration or revelation. All too frequently the skeptic uses only one or two of the sources cited above. In reality all four are needed if one is to understand the "whole truth." As Lowell Bennion once remarked: "No single avenue of knowledge has given us the whole truth about life. No one single approach to truth can stand alone. We need them all to supplement one another and to verify one another as much as it is possible for them to do. Knowledge, which appeals to our minds, warms our hearts, is verified in experience, and is attested to by trustworthy witnesses in their respective fields, is most certainly part of the truth we seek."

But there are some truths that can only be verified by the Spirit (revelation). As one reads the scriptures he can come to know spiritual truth in private communication with the Lord. As he seeks with a sincere heart the answer comes, very seldom in an audible voice, but usually through the still, small voice of the Comforter. This Comforter—the Holy Ghost—clarifies the mind and causes one to know and feel.

People everywhere are searching and seeking and yet can't find God. Jesus said: "Ask, and it shall be given you; seek, and ye shall find; knock, and it shall be opened unto you:

"For every one that asketh receiveth; and he that seeketh findeth; and to him that knocketh it shall be opened." (Matthew 7:7–8.)

But he also observed, through his prophet Isaiah, "For as the heavens are higher than the earth, so are my ways higher than your ways, and my thoughts than your thoughts" (Isaiah 55:9).

To me this scripture implies, in the case of the seeking of a truth, that, though we seek with faith, humility, and sincerity and thus will receive answers, those answers may not always come exactly the way or in the time frame we might expect. The Lord will choose the method and time according to his knowledge of us and our ultimate needs and circumstances.

A religion professor shared this experience:

"Tommy turned out to be the 'atheist in residence' in my course. He constantly objected to or smirked at the possibility of an unconditionally loving God. We lived with each other in relative peace for one semester although at times he was a pain in the neck. At the end of the course when he turned in his final exam, he asked in a slightly cynical tone, 'Do you think I'll ever find God?' I decided on a little shock therapy. 'No!' I said emphatically. 'Oh,' he responded, 'I thought that was the product you were pushing.' I let him get five steps from the door and then called out, 'Tommy! I don't think you'll

ever find him, but I am certain he will find you!'
Tommy shrugged and left. I felt slightly disappointed
that he had missed my clever line.

"Later I heard that Tom had graduated and I was
duly grateful. Then came a sad report: Tommy had
developed terminal cancer. Before I could search him
out, he came to me. When he walked into my office,
his body was badly wasted, and his long hair had
fallen out because of chemotherapy. But his eyes
were bright and his voice was firm, for the first time, I
think. 'Tommy, I've thought about you so often. I
hear you are sick!' I blurted out.

" 'Oh, yes, very sick. I have cancer. It's a matter
of weeks.'

" 'Can you talk about it?'

" 'Sure, what would you like to know?'

" 'What's it like to be only twenty-four and know
that you're dying?'

" 'Well, it could be worse.'

" 'Like what?'

" 'Well, like being fifty and having no values or
ideals,' Tom said. 'Like being fifty and thinking that
booze and making money are the real "biggies" in
my life.

" 'But what I really came to see you about is something you said to me on the last day of class. I asked if
you thought I would ever find God and you said,
"No!" which surprised me. Then you said, "But he
will find you." I thought about that a lot, even
though my search for God was hardly intense at that
time.' (My 'clever' line. He thought about that a lot!)

" 'But when the doctors removed a lump from my
groin and told me that it was malignant, I got serious
about locating God. And when the malignancy
spread into my vital organs, I really began banging
against the bronze doors of heaven. But nothing

happened. Well, one day I woke up and, instead of throwing a few more futile appeals to a God who may or may not be there, I just quit. I decided I didn't really care about God, an afterlife, or anything like that.

" 'I decided to spend what time I had left doing something more profitable. I thought about you and something else you had said: "The essential sadness is to go through life without loving. But it would be almost equally sad to leave this world without ever telling those you loved that you had loved them." So I began with the hardest one: my dad. He was reading the newspaper when I approached him.'

" 'Dad, I would like to talk with you.'

" 'Well, talk.'

" 'I mean, it's really important.'

"The newspaper came down three slow inches. 'What is it?'

" 'Dad, I love you. I just wanted you to know that.'

"Tom smiled at me and said with obvious satisfaction, as though he felt a warm and secret joy flowing inside him, 'The newspaper fluttered to the floor. Then my father did two things I couldn't remember him doing before. He cried and he hugged me. And we talked all night, even though he had to go to work the next morning.

" 'It was easier with my mother and little brother. They cried with me, too, and we hugged one another, and we shared the things we had been keeping secret for so many years. I was only sorry that I had waited so long. Here I was, in the shadow of death, and I was just beginning to open up to all the people I had actually been close to.

" 'Then one day I turned around and God was there. He didn't come to me when I pleaded with him. Apparently God does things in his own way and at his own hour. The important thing is that you were right. He found me even after I stopped looking for him.'

'' 'Tom, could I ask you a favor? Would you come to my theology-of-faith course and tell my students what you just told me?'

"Though we scheduled a date he never made it.

"Before he died, we talked one last time. 'I'm not going to make it to your class,' he said.

'' 'I know, Tom.'

'' 'Will you tell them for me? Will you . . . tell the whole world for me?'

'' 'I will, Tom. I'll tell them.' '' (John Powell, "Tell the World for Me" [Allen, Texas: S. J. Argus Communication].)

Faith, or the discovery of God, cannot be found in a theology class or a textbook. As in Tommy's case, it has to be experienced, reasoned, and verified by the Spirit.

The person of faith has the assurance that he is living and striving for ideals that will never perish but are certain to become an increasingly large aspect of the universe. He lives his moral life with more hope and happiness than the equally fine person who is lacking such faith.

W. P. Montague said: "If God is not, then the existence of all that is beautiful and in any sense good, is but the accidental and ineffective by-product of blindly swirling atoms, or of the equally unpurposeful, though more conceptually complicated, mechanisms of present-day physics. A man may well believe that this dreadful thing is true. For to wish there should be no God is to wish that the things we love and strive to realize and make permanent, should be only temporary and doomed to frustration and destruction. If life and its fulfillments are good, why should one rejoice in the news that God is dead and that there is nothing in the whole world but our frail and perishable selves that is concerned with anything that matters? Not that such a prospect would diminish the duty to make the best of what we have while we have it. Goodness is not made less good by a lack of cosmic support for it. Morality is sanctionless and can never derive its validity from what is external to itself and to the life whose fulfillment it is. Atheism leads not to badness but only to an incurable sadness and loneliness.''

For Tommy and others like him I remind us all that ''he that findeth his life shall lose it: and he that loseth his life for my sake shall find it'' (Matthew 10:39).

If there are questions in our minds concerning God's existence, let us study the great minds and the experiences of others. Let us use our own minds in logical thinking and good judgment. Also, we should remember that one of the most trustworthy avenues to truth lies in the laboratory of experience. In the affairs of everyday life, we learn to trust experience. But perhaps the most vital of all our pursuits is to seek the Spirit.

''If any of you lack wisdom, let him ask of God, that giveth to all men liberally, and upbraideth not; and it shall be given him'' (James 1:5).

To this I add my own witness and testimony—it is so!